A DISSERTATION UPON THE POLITICAL HISTORY OF THE ELEPHANT

W. AUGUSTUS SCHLEGEL

FULL WELL VENTURES

A Dissertation upon the Political History of the Elephant

By Schlegel, W. Augustus

Originally published as a series of articles in 1823-24 issues of *The Newcastle Magazine*

CONTENTS

Chapter I	1
Chapter II	11
Chapter III	21
Chapter IV	33
Chapter V	50
Chapter VI	64

CHAPTER I

NOVEMBER 1823

THE POSSESSION of the elephant, as the most powerful of all beasts of burden, has promoted the commercial activity and increased the warlike powers of states; in the course of innumerable wars the elephants have been the allies of man, in the southern parts of Asia from the most remote times, and for some centuries back in the countries bordering upon the Mediterranean sea. The art of taming the elephant, and particularly of breaking him in for war, has been practiced in India from times beyond the reach of authentic history, and there it was originally and exclusively indigenous. When in later ages the same thing was undertaken in various countries of Africa, it was done in imitation of what had been learnt in India, and that not by the natives of those countries, who had neither means nor inclination, but by people in a higher state of civilization who had settled in that part of the world.

In natural history the African elephant has been generally confounded with the Indian; and it is but lately that a celebrated philosopher has pointed out with scientific precision the essential difference between the two kinds of the same genus. The ancients, however, knew that the Indian elephant excelled the African in size, strength, and courage, at least in those parts of Africa with which they were acquainted. The Indian elephant has certainly obtained a higher renown, because it has been for thousands of years the countryman, as it were, of the Indians, who were able to appreciate its abilities, and who possessed a lively sense not only of the beautiful but also of the formidable productions of nature. The Indian Mythology is the only one known to us in which the elephant occupies a considerable place, and in which a kind of apotheosis has been assigned to it. In the architectural monuments of India we find it represented not only in bas and alt relief, but it is intimately interwoven with the ornaments, and bears huge masses of stone as a colossal caryatid. The old heroic songs celebrate the elephant as the habitual companion of kings and heroes, and his gigantic form is ever present to the imagination of the poet.—Many favorite images are borrowed from thence, proverbial phrases betray a familiar acquaintance with the half-reasoning properties of the animal, and even the various appellations bestowed upon it indicate a certain veneration, and perhaps a sort of secret feeling of the rank which the elephant might formerly have possessed amongst living creatures under a different constitution of our planet. The African elephant, on the contrary, dwells partly in unexplored wilds; he finds in the lion of the desert a more worthy opponent than in the timid savage, whose wretched hut he treads underfoot without being aware of it. The Indian elephant is an Achilles who has found his Homers; to the African may be applied the complaint of Alexander the Great, that the deeds of the hero are lost without the mead of the poet's lay.

In our western world the elephant has only become lately

known, but in a more distinguished manner. The most judicious and keen-sighted observer has introduced him into science, the noblest among conquerors, into the art of war; and the knowledge of this distinguished and, in his kind, unique animal is forever united with the names of Aristotle and Alexander. In the following centuries also, when the elephants appeared in greater numbers upon the stage of history, the mention of them is generally connected with the memory of the most remarkable men and the most decisive events.

To begin, then, in the first place, with the oldest of our ancients, it is extremely well worth remarking that in the Egyptian monuments not the slightest trace appears of an acquaintance with the elephant, though in the neighboring country, Upper Ethiopia, it always was, and still is, indigenous.[1] We shall presently speak of the elephant hunting of the Ptolemies: the Praetorians, whom Nero had sent out to explore Ethiopia, returned word that they had found traces of elephants immediately above Meroë.—(Plin. Hist. Nat. 1. 6, c. 19.)—The Egyptian priests were very observant of all natural productions which could be either serviceable or prejudicial to man; and one would suppose that in the enormous edifices which the Egyptians were in the habit of constructing, they would have found such a beast of burden very useful where they had to transport great masses of stone by land, and they could easily have supported them in their great abundance of grain. But setting aside the possibility of taming the elephant, how came it that they did not imitate in stone the striking and gigantic figure, by which it was known to them, and introduce it as an appropriate ornament into their temples and palaces? Or use it as an emblem in their hieroglyphics? Egypt was fortunately poor in wild beasts.—(Herod II, c. 65.)—The few which it possessed are variously represented in bas-relief in her architectural monuments; not only the crocodile and hippopotamus, but also the rarer animals, the wolf and jackal. Amongst the Egyptian sculptures is to be found the true and not to be mistaken image of the giraffe. This animal could only have been brought into Egypt as a show; though, indeed, being defenseless and not adapted for flight, it was more easily caught by the savage inhabitants of inner Africa than the formidable elephant. In Egypt itself there were no lions; the lion hunting which we see so elegantly represented on the walls of the royal palace of Thebes (Descript. De l'Egypte, Antiquite's t. II, planche 9,) must be supposed to have taken place on the Libyan frontier; and yet the lion was, in its solitary form or paired with others, a favorite subject of ancient Egyptian sculpture. These lions, and among others those in the Diocletian baths at Rome, are of such excellent workmanship, the individuality so happily expressed, that they suppose in the artist a calm and continued observation of the living animal. Without doubt the Egyptian kings kept lions in their menageries, and if so, why not also elephants, as a foreign and wonderful variety, if they had been accessible to them?

It is allowed on all hands, that the cultivation of Egypt has followed the course of the Nile; and, perhaps, we must assign to this cultivation so ancient a date as to suppose that it kept pace with the geological formation of the land. As the lower vale of the Nile rose from the morass by the successive overflowings of the river, human population appears to have followed close upon it. But opinions are divided as to the geographical point from which the civilization of Egypt (properly so called) took its rise. Many enquirers would wish to refer everything to Ethiopia; but perhaps this view of the subject is hardly tenable. Many circumstances seem to indicate that the intellectual horizon of the Egyptians was extremely circumscribed on the side of Ethiopia. Otherwise one must maintain that they had totally forgotten the original seat and source of their civilization, in a country, too, closely adjoining, and not separated from them by any impassable gulf, which, in a people so careful in preserving all their old traditions, is nowise credible.—Their want of acquaintance with the elephant seems to throw no inconsiderable weight into the scale of the arguments which may be adduced on both sides.

Much earlier than the elephant itself, the costly spoil won from the vanquished beast, the ivory was known in the countries within whose bounds our ancient history is circumscribed. Of this we may find a trace in the geography of Egypt, in the name of the city Elephantine, placed in an island of the Nile, over against Syene. It is clear, that all the Grecian appellatives of Egyptian cities were given them before the time of Alexander the Great, either by the Ionians, who settled in Egypt under Psammetichus, or by the race of interpreters who derived from that settlement: and we may boldly assume that the Grecian name expressed the sense of the indigenous appellation. But we must not suppose that by Elephantine is meant the city of elephants (for what could elephants have to do with a rocky island of the Nile), but the city of ivory. Nothing is more natural than that the inhabitants of Upper Ethiopia should come to this southern boundary of Egypt to barter their elephants' teeth for other wares. The judicious Bochart (Hierozoic, 1. II. C. 23.) considers Elephantine as synonymous with Philae, as if the latter, which is the Egyptian name of the place, had been translated into the former. From this it would incontestably follow that the elephant, or at least that ivory, had introduced even into Egypt a name widely known throughout the east. Herodotus makes no mention of Philae, but only of the city Elephantine; Strabo, who had visited the country, distinguishes the two very accurately; Elephantine lay below the cataracts; Philae, above them, upon the road, at the distance of a hundred stadia, also on an island of the Nile. Meantime, it is not improbable that both places, on account of their similar destination as staples of the Ethiopian trade, bore the same name. The Ethiopians might sail down the Nile as far as Philae; there it would be necessary, on account of the cataracts, to unload the wares and bring them by land to Elephantine, where they might be reshipped. One may suppose that the Ionians would give a name to the nearer city in their own language, and leave its Egyptian name to Philae, which was seldomer visited. Monsieur Jomard, in his excellent description of Elephantine, agrees with Bochart that Philae and Elephantine were synonymous in the Greek and Egyptian languages, and were applied as a joint name to the whole groups of islands near the cataracts. He endeavors to show by ingenious arguments, that by the name Elephantine, Herodotus understood the city which Strabo calls Philae.— The intricate passage in Pliny is rather favorable than otherwise to this opinion, and so Bochart would be in some degree right.

And here we must not overlook that the word 'elephas,' which the Romans inherited from the Greeks, and from them, the more modern people of Europe, does not in Greek originally signify the elephant, but simply ivory.—In the latter sense it is often used in Homer, and once in Hesiod, and proves that the Greeks of that age, from eight to nine hundred years before our era, were well acquainted with ivory. They understood the art of sawing it and turning it (Od. viii. 404, 405, xix. 56.)—The Macedonian and Carian women stained it with spots of purple, by which its dazzling whiteness was heightened; and so ornamented it was used as a cheek piece in the bridles of horses (Il. iv. 141 sq.). The bridal bed of Ulysses, the chair of Penelope was inlaid with it; the palace of Menelaus shone with gold, silver, amber, and ivory (Od. xix. 55 sq., xxiii. 200, iv. 73). Although it was reckoned a costly variety, it must have been employed in considerable masses, if the poet could represent a whole gate, though only an emblematical one, as covered with it (Od. xix. 562-565).

There is little room to doubt what nation it was through whose intervention ivory was introduced so early into Greece. But it is by no means an uninteresting question, with respect to the intercourse of nations, whether the Phoenicians brought the ivory, which they traded with in Asia Minor and Greece, from Africa and India. All probabilities are in favor of the former supposition. It is not to be denied that there was some channel by which commerce found its way from India to the western world, latterly, perhaps, by Colchis and the Black Sea; but this channel could hardly be through Persia at that period, because, as we shall soon see, till the time of Darius Hystaspes, the Persians were entirely unacquainted with India Proper. Besides, we have express testimony that the ships of King Solomon sailed in company with those of the Phoenicians from the Arabic gulf to the land of Ophir, to import with other expensive rarities, abundance of ivory for his splendid throne and the buildings of his temple; and Ophir is, according to the more probable opinion of the commentators, a part of the eastern cost of Africa, perhaps Sofala or Mozambique. Finally, it appears from the nature of things that Africa could always furnish more ivory for foreign trade than India.

In Asia, the elephant is only indigenous on the south of the great mountain chain, in the two Indian peninsulas and the adjacent islands. From the dense population of these countries his native range is confined to those regions, which either have not been reached by cultivation, or where nature has opposed to this cultivation insurmountable obstacles; to the mountain vales and the irreligious woodlands at the foot of the mountain. In Africa, on the contrary, the elephant abounds from the Cape of Good Hope, where the European settlements have only driven him a little back, along the western coast as far as Senegal, along the eastern coast, with a few interruptions, to Abyssinia; and than through Nigritia, across through the whole of this quarter of the globe. —One need only cast his eye over the map to see how the district of Asia already mentioned suddenly contracts to a point. How far the elephant spreads into the interior of Africa, we know not; but it cannot be denied the requisites exist there for the prosperity of the race; for although the mouths of no great rivers appear upon the coast, they must exist, and lose themselves in lakes, or sink into the sand.

The taming of the elephant from time immemorial, so far from increasing the quantity of ivory, would rather tend to make it scarcer. For the value of the teeth of the animal when slain, bears no proportion to the worth of the living one, when broken in for some important purpose. The hunting of the elephant in India appears to have been a royal prerogative, and carried on with a certain forbearance so as not to diminish the breed.

Add to this, that the Indians, in the age to which our oldest accounts of the Asiatic trade reach back, were undoubtedly in possession of all the conveniences of life, and consequently, that an extensive home consumption would diminish the exportation. In the Amara-Kosha, a book probably written above two thousand years ago, ivory is described as the common material out of which puppets were carved for children. But it is wherewith a material consideration, that the African elephants are much more liberally provided with ivory than the Indian. In Africa, the long tusks are common to both sexes, while in India the tusks of the females only reach to a few inches (La Menagérie du Museum National d'Histoire Naturelle par Lacipede, Cuvier et Geoffroi. T. 1, p. 95). In Ceylon, which for ages has been famed for its strong and warlike elephants, there is a numerous variety in which the tusks, without discrimination of sex, are altogether wanting. Since Cuvier, the natural historian, who first explained the characteristic distinction between the two kinds of elephants, especially from the internal structure of the grinders, leaves it at least doubtful, whether the African elephants do not shed their tusks as well as their grinders at certain periods, it may be allowable to quote the express affirmative testimony of a Grecian author. Aelian says that the elephants in Mauritania shed their horns, as he calls the tusks, every ten years (History Animal, 1, xiv, c. 5). —Unfortunately he does not give his authority (if it were from the writings of King Juba, some weight might belong to the assertion); but, like an injudicious collector, he accompanies the assertion with so many absurd tales, that they would throw doubt upon the most credible facts. Meantime, it is well known that not nearly all the ivory exported from Africa is got from slain elephants, but that many tusks are found in the woods (Shaw's zoology, v. 1, p. 213); and this circumstance gives to the statement an additional degree of probability. The matter deserves the investigation of future travelers.

The acute and tasteful historian of the Grecian Toreutic, or the art of making carved work from the noble metals, fine wood, ivory, and other costly materials, Monsieur Quatremere-de-Quincy, was led in the course of his investigations to the ivory trade among the ancients. He asserts, that at the time when Phidias covered the naked parts of his colossal statues entirely with ivory, this article had become abundant in Greece; that in the course of some centuries it became gradually scarcer, and must become still scarcer from the decrease of the species. The later accounts of travelers in Africa do not confirm this apprehension. According as the article was more or less in demand, and more or fewer markets were open for its sale, the price of ivory might rise or fall; but upon the whole the proportion would remain the same.

---

1. Belzoni tells us that he found the image of an elephant sculptured on one of the temples of Philae, but this was probably of date posterior to the age of Ptolemies.

CHAPTER II

DECEMBER 1823

A LTHOUGH AT present the art of sculpture nowhere
creates a particular demand for ivory, it may be
doubted whether the importation in modern Europe is not
larger than it was among the civilized nations of the ancient
western world. The quantity of ivory which the Greeks
consumed in works of art borders upon the incredible; but to
procure it required great cost and exertion: and the master
pieces of Phidias and Polycletus excited general admiration,
not only on account of their inimitable beauty but on account
of the costliness of the materials. This expense, however, was
made once for all: such a work remained unimpaired for
hundreds of years. —On the contrary, thousands of small
tools and pieces of furniture, which in modern Europe serve
for the most ordinary purposes, wear away, and require to be
constantly renewed. In Rome, in the last years of the republic
and the first of the empire, two causes cooperated to produce
an immoderate consumption, the pomp of the public monuments and an unbounded private luxury. Then, also,
happened that extraordinary concurrence of circumstances
mentioned by Pliny, a temporary dearness and scarcity, espe-

cially of the large teeth, which could only be procured in India. —(Hist. Nat. 1. viii, c. 3.) The commercial relations of the Romans reached mediately as far as the further Peninsula, which, even at this day, especially in Pegu and Cochinchina, produces teeth of uncommon size. —(Shaw Zool. V. 1, p. 313 sq.)[1] Quatremere de Quincy has, it seems, drawn a too general conclusion with respect to those remote times, and misinterpreted a passage of Pliny. Pliny speaks here only of the extraordinary size of the Indian elephants, not of their teeth; we have seen that the conclusion upon the one point is not valid as to the other. At present the greatest quantity of ivory, and, as we are assured by the most competent judges, the London dealers in ivory, the best in quality comes from Africa. —(Shaw Zool. V. 1, p. 224.) From all that has been said above, and from several circumstances hereafter to be mentioned, this must have been still more the case in ancient times, at least till the age of Alexander the Great, by whose conquests India became better known and more accessible. It admits, then, of little doubt that the gigantic works in sculpture of Phidias and Polycletus were composed of African ivory.

We need not in this case pay much attention to the expressions of the poets. For the sake of amplifying, they called any remote land from which ivory came, sometimes India, Ethiopia, or Mauritania, as it happened to suit their fancy or the metre of their verse. Many instances might be quoted from the Roman poets of the Augustan age, but they only show that the names of all places producing ivory were familiar to them. The question must be decided by other reasons and authorities. We find ivory spoken of in Italy in very early times, though not by contemporary authors. The Romans borrowed the custom of using curule chairs from the Etruscans, and these latter probably received the ivory necessary for that purpose from the Phoenicians settled in Africa, namely, the

Carthaginians; for it does not appear that the Etruscans extended their navigation in early times over the western basin of the Mediterranean sea.

It gives rise to some reflections, when one considers that the contemporaries of Pericles, who looked with such an intelligent admiration at the Pallas in the Parthenon and the Olympian Jupiter, and even the artist themselves either had no notion or a very erroneous one of the animal from whose teeth or horns (for they did not agree upon that point) those wonderful statues of the Gods were composed. It appears that the highest genius and skill in the arts was not incompatible with great deficiency in geographical and physical knowledge, and we have daily experience that the contrary is equally possible.

Herodotus is the oldest of the Grecian historians who have reached our times, in whose writings the word 'elephas' is used to signify the elephant. But it is only the bare mention of the animal without any description; according to all appearance, the historian, notwithstanding his extensive travels, had never himself seen it. He divides the northern coast of Africa into two halves, he describes the eastern Libya, inhabited by Nomads, as flat and sandy. Westward from this river, on the contrary, the country becomes mountainous and woody, having a great variety and abundance of wild beasts, and amongst others the elephant. —(Herod, 1. iv, c. 191.) If the testimony of Herodotus stood single one might suspect a mistake, because, in our days, in these districts, the piratical states of Fez and Morocco, there is no trace whatever of the elephant. But we shall see enough to convince us that much later, in times of authentic history, the elephants existed there in abundance, and we shall be able to unravel the causes which have extirpated the race in the north of the great desert.

The account which Herodotus gives of the mustering of

the army with which Xerxes invaded Greece, is a remarkable document. Exaggeration and mistakes may very naturally have crept into it; but we have, on the contrary, no reason to apprehend omissions, especially of the surprising and marvelous, as the Greeks would take every pain to magnify their victories.—From this military review it appears incontestable that the kings of Persia possessed at that time no war-elephants, for, if Xerxes had possessed them, he would not have left them behind in a campaign to which he summoned all his strength, and in which the Arabs appeared upon their camels as an extraordinary kind of cavalry. —Aeschylus, an eyewitness of the events, is silent likewise about the elephants in the army of Xerxes, although he differs from Herodotus in many particulars—a circumstance which ought not to surprise us, as the same exactness and minuteness is not required from a poet as from an historian.

Again, it follows, from the absence of war-elephants, that no Indian prince was then in subjection to the Persian monarchy, although Darius boasted of the great conquests he had made in India. Among the pretended Indians of Herodotus we must not conceive that there were any real Indians, speaking Sanskrit, or any dialect derived from it, and living under the Braminical system of government, but savage hordes, negro-like Autochthones upon the right bank of the Indus, in modern Candabar and Baluchistan. We can hardly tell rightly what to think of the ships of discovery which Darius sent out upon the Indus, as, in speaking of this river, it is said to take a false direction to the east. So far is evident, if Herodotus tells us correctly what the Persians of his time knew of India, they knew nothing of it at all, and we are justified in concluding that not the least intercourse existed between these adjoining countries. Judging from their language, we must, according to Sir W. Jones, consider the Persians and Indians as nearly related nations, which at some remote time had wandered from a common primitive settlement. But, as it appears, they knew nothing more of each other, and at a later period became again acquainted as strangers.

Nature, it is true, has placed a strong barrier between the two countries: mountains towards the north, further down the course of the river, and of the vale which it waters, large deserts. The district where Alexander passed the Indus has been the inlet, through which most of the late conquerors have made their entrance, and here the five large rivers of the Punjab opposed a considerable obstacle.

From this ignorance of the Persians respecting India, it follows further, that the Phoenician navigation from the Arabian Gulf had not reached India at so early a date; for otherwise Darius would have been able to obtain better information from the Phoenicians, who belonged to his empire, and were compelled to assist him with their shipping.

As far as we know, Ctesias, who lived perhaps sixty years after Herodotus, was the first Greek who gave a circumstantial description of the elephant from personal inspection. But his disregard of truth is sufficiently notorious, and in his description of this wonderful animal he maintained his usual character. Aristotle contradicts his account sometimes with the mention of his name, (Arist. de Animal. Hist. l. iii, c. 22, in fine,) once he only quotes the old saying, but in such a manner that the insinuation can only apply to Ctesias, (Aristot. de Animal, ingressu, c. 9,) whose writings, though composed not above half a century before, were yet the oldest which the Grecians had upon this subject.

Ctesias was a favorite author of his countrymen on account of his agreeable style, and perhaps, also, on account of his dealing so much in the marvelous. For the Grecians had an amiable partiality to embrace an error, when dressed up with the embellishments of imagination, and parted from it very unwillingly, if the sober truth was exhibited to them ever so plainly. There is, perhaps, no other instance of a people so ingenious who allowed themselves to be imposed upon by such absurdities. It is only for this reason that the writings of Ctesias, which are lost, deserve mention, for his book upon India became the great magazine for all subsequent fictitious accounts of travels. It was there that we have men with dogs' heads, headless men with their face in their breast, nimble runners with one leg, the flat-footed race of men who laid themselves upon their bellies and backs and stretched up their large feet as umbrellas, and many other things of the same sort, which have been transplanted in the Pseudo-Callisthenes, the Legend of St. Brandanus, the Travels of Sinbad and Maundeville, and those of Duke Ernst of Germany.

Together with this idle abuse of the imagination, which Ctesias introduced among writers and readers who never heard his name, his writings had a more serious consequence in the History of the World: for there can be no doubt that the reading of them inflamed the mind of Alexander the Great with that irresistible desire to penetrate into and subdue this land of wonders; and although his rapidly acquired possession of some provinces upon the borders was soon lost, his campaign had the weightiest consequences.

India was not now so inaccessible to the Persians as before, and some political and commercial intercourse began to take place. Indian princes sent presents to the kings of Persia, after the eastern fashion. Those mentioned by Ctesias are of such a kind that he could not have invented them. — Among other honorary presents was the elephant, which Ctesias saw at Babylon tear up a palm tree by the roots. This is for once, contrary to the practice of the narrator, something quite credible, and according to the habits of the animal. There can be little doubt that Ctesias had seen the animal, though his account is in many particulars so framed as if he had written only from hearsay. Who else but himself could have spread the childish mistake that the elephant has no joints in his legs, and, therefore, sleeps leaning against a tree, and that the tree is sawn in such a way above the roots, by the hunters, as just to be able to support itself, and falls when the elephant rests against it; and that when the elephant has once fallen to the ground, not being able to rise again, he is easily taken. Upon the last point Aristotle disdains to enlarge; the first assertion he refutes, and describes exactly how the elephant walks, and how he lays himself down. —(Arist. de Animal ingressa, c. 9—Histor. Anim. 1. ii, c. 1.) It is well known that the animal loves to roll himself upon his back, and rises again with great nimbleness from this position; and in the wild state, notwithstanding its bulk, bounds high into the air.

Ctesias, then, the first among the Greeks, had learnt what an important part the elephant performed in the Indian art of war. He positively asserts having heard (and here he may be believed) that one hundred thousand elephants marched in front of the king of India (as if there were only one king) and that three thousand were kept in the rear, and used in sieges to batter the walls. This statement goes far beyond the bounds not only of all authentic historical facts, but beyond the highest number which has been reckoned by Indian writers upon the art of war as the complement of an army. —The possibility of bringing together and maintaining so many elephants can only be supposed in the case that the whole peninsula of Hindustan was under the dominion of one master, which it certainly was not at the time of Ctesias, and several centuries before.

Diodorus has, besides, preserved one story of Ctesias, (Diodor. Sic. 1. 11, c. 16-19,) by which this is proved, if nothing else, that the narrator was well informed of the effect and the terror inspired by the elephant in war. Semiramis is going to undertake a campaign against Stabrobates, an Indian king: but as she had no elephants, she causes to be slain three hundred thousand black oxen, their skins to be secretly sewed up, and stuffed with straw in the shape of elephants. She sets these masks upon so many camels. She crosses the Indus; the sight of the reputed elephants, at a distance, excites a great terror at first among the Indians, who believed themselves to be the only possessors of these animals. But deserters soon betray the secret. The Indian cavalry now pushes boldly on, but is soon thrown into confusion by the unusual appearance and smell of the camels. Hereupon Stabrobates orders his infantry to advance in regular line of battle; the elephants placed in front press forward with resistless force, and cause great havoc: Semiramis herself, wounded, takes to flight, and her whole army retires across the Indus. The heroic queen lost in this battle two-thirds of her army, which consisted of three thousand infantry, five hundred thousand cavalry, and one hundred thousand war chariots. —This is a short abstract of the narrative; which is embellished with so many particular circumstances, as if the narrator had himself been present at the campaign. A question here arises, has Ctesias invented all this out of his own head? Or has he drawn the materials of his narrative from the Persian archives, which he boasted of having access to? If we adopted the latter supposition, have we here the historical account of a real event? —or do we read a portion of a mythological heroic poem upon the celebrated empress of the east? —or, finally, did Ctesias meet with this marvelous history not in Persia but in India? These four suppositions seem more or less allied to probability according to the order in which they are placed.

The story is too marvelous for a contemporary description; as an heroic mythological poem, not sufficiently glorious for the heroine. There seems little hesitation, then, in referring to no other authority than the brain of Ctesias, as he cannot be freed from the charge of having purposely falsified for the amusement of his readers. If, on the contrary, this fabulous writer had found any documents in the Persian archives to serve as the groundwork of his narrative, it would contain a confession that, in times of remote antiquity, fruitless attempts had been made by the Assyrian or Medo-Persian kings to conquer India, and that the Indian art of war had been superior to that practiced in the western kingdoms of Asia, more especially in consequence of the use of elephants.

The battle between the king Artaxerxes Mnemon and the younger Cyrus, in which Ctesias was present, and attended the wounded monarch, is described minutely by Xenophon, who was engaged in the action; and from his account it clearly appears that Artaxerxes had no war elephants. With this account we may also compare the passage at the end of the Cyropaedia, where Xenophon describes the condition of the Persian armaments, as they were in his time, and particularizes the component parts, cavalry, and infantry, and scythed chariots. His silence concerning elephants is here quite decisive. (Cyrop. 1. viii, c. 8, in fin.)

The elephants which come before us in a credible form in our Universal History, are those at the battle of Arbela. Although Darius Codomanus came in person to meet Alexander at the gates of his kingdom upon the Issus, he had brought no elephants with him; they were reserved as an irreparable bodyguard for the last extremity, and, in the decisive engagement, stood together with the noblest Persian knights, immediately before the war chariot of the great king. (Arrian, 1, iii, c. xi, also c. ix. 1l.) In the battle at Arbela, frequent mention is made of Indians, but in the improper sense, as in the review of Xerxes: they were, according to the express observation of the most authentic narrator, inhabitants of the right bank of the Indus, who had brought with them those elephants, amounting to only fifteen in number. (1b. c. viii. 1l.) Small as this number is, it proves, nevertheless, either that the immediate predecessors of Darius Codomanus had subjugated provinces on this side of the Indus, which, in the time of Xerxes, and perhaps also that of Artaxerxes Mnemon, did not belong to the Persian empire; or that a change had taken place in the arming and military art of the dependent Indian tribes, which can only be attributed to the newly established intercourse with the states of India Proper, on the eastern side of the Indus.

---

1. Jupiter Olympien, p. 167. Voilii pourquot l' on recherchait les plus grandes defenses. Selon Pline on les trouvait dans l'Inde. The passage in Pliny at full length is this: Indicum (elephant Afri pavent, nec contuerf audent: nam et major Indicis magnitudo est.

CHAPTER III

JANUARY 1824

SINCE, THEN, according to the unanimous statement of the Grecian contemporaries and eyewitnesses of the events, a small beginning of the use of war elephants first took place in the Persian armies, when the dynasty of the Achaemenidae was overthrown, (331 A. Chr.) we are enabled to form an opinion as to the authenticity of the traditions of the modern Persians, who refer this usage to a very remote antiquity. According to Firdassi, Feridun was the first who tamed elephants and broke them in for war, and Feridun, or Feridoun, is explained to be the Median Arbaces of the Greeks, who lived 800 years before our era. —(Sir John Malcolm's History of Persia, vol. 1, p. 24.) Was Feridoun, we may ask, at the same time master of India, or were these wild elephants in Iran? Persian vanity would perhaps make no hesitation to assert the first, but evidence is wanting. The three sons of Feridoun evidently represent emblematically three great nations: —Salm, the Aramaic tribes in the west; Tur, the Nomads to the north; and Irai, the youngest favorite, the Persians themselves. No member of the family appears as the representative of India. This is so much the more striking, as the Persians and Indians, from their language, must be considered as brothers, while, on the contrary, the other tribes are decidedly of a distinct race. But the Persian dominion had at times stretched itself over the whole of western Asia and part of Tartary—never over India. It is true that the Dabistan speaks of a very ancient Persic-Indian monarchy, but this book is of recent date, and of no sufficient authority, and does not invalidate the conclusion that, as far as our history reaches, Persia and India were always separate and independent of each other, and we may safely assume that Mahmud Ghaznerides was the first who really conquered India with a Persian army. We are further told in the Shahnameh, that Rastan, the popular hero of Persian proverbs, contemporary of Kai Kaaus, (according to Sir John Malcolm, the Cyaxares of the Greeks) when he conquered Mazenderan, slew a great number of elephants. The most recent and very respectable historian of Persia, whose authority is entitled to consideration, as having traveled in the country, and from his acquaintance with the language, being able to compre the native traditions with the testimony of the ancients, concludes from thence, somewhat too boldly perhaps, that the elephant was formerly abundant in Persia. He appeals both to the history of the country and the monuments of sculpture; and remarks that Mazenderan, the Hyrcania of the ancients, upon the southern shore of the Caspian Sea, is, by its climate and abundant vegetation, more favorable than any other province of Persia to the thriving of the species. (Hist. of Persia, vol. 1, p. 35. It is not easy to reconcile with this assertion what the author says, vol. 2, p. 515. It is not probable that the elephant was ever indigenous to Persia: but there is no doubt that from the most early times, they were known and used in war by its inhabitants. The last proposition has, I trust, been sufficiently refuted.) —There is, no doubt, a possibility in favor of the supposition, for animals have been transplanted by man with success, showing that nature has not distributed the living kinds in all places where they could thrive. The poets often talk of Hyrcanian tigers, but no geographer, so far as we know, has ever mentioned elephants wild and indigenous in Hyrcania. The greatest part of the country between the Euphrates and the Indus, on account of its dry air and want of water, would hardly suit the wild living elephant; to which the district of Mazenderan may be an exception. We have seen how the matter stands with respect to the testimony of authentic history. As to the Persian monuments of sculpture, we may consider it as an infallible proof that they are later than the days of Alexander the Great, if elephants are represented upon them.

We must now return once more to the elephants captured at the battle of Arbela, for though the number was but small, they become important to the historical enquirer by several concurrent circumstances. In the first place, these animals formed as it were, the first kernel of those new squadrons which, in a short time, spread themselves over the whole western world from the Indus to the Pyrenees; and secondly, we have every reason to believe that some of them were the very animals upon which Aristotle made his observations. It is clear that the philosopher could have written his book upon animals only in the last years of his life. He might, perhaps, have turned his attention to the animal world in earlier years, but he was then confined to the native species of Greece. The campaigns of Alexander first opened to him the living deeds of remote climates: the natural historian had need of a conqueror to deliver into his hands as a scientific spoil the rare and hitherto unknown productions of nature. We know how nobly Alexander met his instructor's thirst for knowledge: he expended not only large sums, and placed some thousands of men, hunters, fishers, bird-catchers, at his command, (Plin. Hist. Natur. 1. viii, c. 16,) but he appears to have neglected no opportunity of procuring for him, by his own personal attention, remarkable subjects.

It was now that Alexander opened his career as a conqueror, by passing over into Asia (Ol. cxi, 8,) twelve years before the death of his instructor, who only survived him two years. In the fourth year after this, (Ol. cxii. 2,) the battle of Arbela took place; and four years later Alexander made his campaign in India, where he got into his possession a great number of elephants. Had the natural historian arranged his work according to the plan of most recent zoologists, who treat of each genus separately, he might without difficulty, have added any newly discovered species. But he intended it as a general comparative physiology of animals, a form which required that he should be completely in possession of his materials before he proceeded to the composition and finishing. —Throughout the whole work, Aristotle seems to have his eye constantly fixed upon the singular properties of the elephant: his remarks upon this animal are dispersed through all his books in such a manner, that it requires no small degree of pains and time to collect them into one body.

The latest editor of Aristotle's natural history, Schneider, has learnedly and acutely considered the question as to the period at which they were composed. After much doubt, he nearly gives up the point of fixing the time very exactly: from a hint in the meteorological books, which, according to his opinion, must have been written at the same time as the zoological, he inclines to think that Aristotle must have written or finished both works after his return to Athens (Ol. cxi. 3,). —But, in this conclusion, he has not sufficiently consulted the natural history of the elephant, which is of considerable moment in fixing the date. In the other articles of his work, Aristotle might have profited by the labors of his predecessors without naming them, but in this he had no other than Ctesias, to whom his enquiring mind could give no credence. Ουχ ων αζιοπιςος is the expression he applies to him. —That the elephant was never seen in Greece before the victories of Alexander, is proved by the express testimony of Pausanias (1. 1, c. xii, 4,). Aristotle might have begun his researches upon the elephant, at soonest, some time after the battle at Arbela, and according to Pausanias, who is followed by Buffon, the elephants conquered from Porus were the first ever brought into Europe, (ab Ol. c. xiii, 2.) The residence of Aristotle at Athens, during the last thirteen years of his life creates no difficulty; with the income he possessed, and what Alexander did for him, he might well have maintained a menagerie near his habitation.

It seems, thence, highly probable, that Alexander sent immediately some of the elephants taken at Arbela to Athens, partly we may suppose, as trophies of his victory, and partly to afford a new and a great gratification to his instructor. We may readily conceive that the active imagination of the youthful conqueror was much struck with the appearance of the animal, and its use in war; he adopted the practice, and in his Indian conquests got possession of as many elephants as he could. But he does not appear to have had leisure enough to collect the most remarkable animals of India. Aristotle mentions the tiger only once, and had certainly never seen it; the rhinoceros remained totally unknown to him.

The elephant, on the contrary, he describes, from his own inspection and continued observation, in both sexes; he speaks of its daily food in Macedonian measures, and was the first who dissected the animal. What he himself could not perceive, its mode of life in the wild state, he gained information of, no doubt, from the Indian drivers, who accompanied the elephants. He must have understood the right method of questioning these people, for they have given him a very intelligent account, and not such tales as Ctesais had either heard or invented. —Aristotle has detailed the bodily structure of the elephant, its motions, its wants, its abilities, in fine, its character and habits in so masterly a manner, and with such distinct outlines, that he has left to future enquirers little to do, except the more exact anatomy of the interior organs; and if we had his entire history of animals, especially his dissections, accompanied with drawings, the gleanings of the moderns, in this department, would perhaps have been very small. A great natural historian has endeavored to set up his own opinion upon some points, in opposition to the authority of Aristotle. The pairing of the elephants, a circumstance very difficult to observe, because in a state of captivity or tameness it only happens occasionally, Aristotle has described very accurately in a few words, as it has been stated by the most recent observers. Buffon raised an objection against his statement, upon anatomical grounds; he was not aware that his objection is set aside by a remarkable physiological appearance in the female elephant, during the rut, which Aristotle describes, and which Monsieur was the first among the modern zoologists to observe again. —(Dehist. Anim. 1. ii, c. i. compare Menagerie du Museum, t. 1, p. 100)—Aristotle asserts that the young elephant sucks with its lip, and not with the proboscis; Persault maintained the contrary; Buffon seized upon that opinion, and thought he had thereby proved his point: both have been refuted by facts. What Aristotle has performed in so new a field of enquiry rises in our estimation, when we compare with it the mistakes which, as if in defiance of him, have been since published by other Greeks, in some instances by those who had been themselves in India. For instance, Onesicritus (Strabon, 1. xvij, p. 103, Amstel.) would extend the life of the elephant to five hundred years, the duration of pregnancy to ten years, while Aristotle has either entirely or nearly hit the right mark. We miss, however, in his books of natural history, which still remain, a striking physiological property of the elephant, namely that he has a small opening near his temples, from which, at certain times, he sweats out a strong smelling moisture. Mr. Wilson, a man of learning, who has lived in India, and rendered considerable services to Sanskrit literature, mentions that Buffon and Shaw have overlooked this circumstance, to which there are frequent allusions in the Indian poets. (The Megadûta, or Cloud Messenger, translated by H.H. Wilson, Calcutta, p. 26, 27.) The excellent description of the elephant by Cuvier had not then reached India, in which this fact is stated. Yet out of India it is anything else than new, for it is mentioned by Strabo, upon the authority of Megasthenes, who is not otherwise famous for talents as an observer, nor for his scrupulous regard to truth. (Strabon, 1. 17. p. 10. 31.) —The above-mentioned natural historian, however, says that this periodical excretion has nothing to do with the rut, and in this he is contradicted by Megasthenes; but by the thousand years' experience of the Indians, which is laid down in the relative expressions of their language, it is probable enough that the appearances which accompany the rut, do not take place so fully and regularly in a colder climate as in the natural abode of the animal.

As on the one hand Alexander introduced the elephant to the researches of science as a wonder of nature, about which truth and error might henceforth contend, so, on the other, he made him an object of ambition to warlike princes and states. This leads us to his Indian campaign, an event infinitely curious, and with respect to which it is difficult to resist the temptation to make digressions, were it only for the purpose of pointing out one single circumstance. This campaign has received the fullest geographical illustrations; in other respects, the recently obtained knowledge of the language, of the old constitution, and manners of the Indians may throw a new light upon the accounts of historians, and serve as a measure of their credibility. But this inquiry must not be entered into episodically.

Alexander made it his first care to subdue the country between Bactria and the Indus, before he ventured to pass the river.[1] The brave tribes whom he met with there, in modern Cabul and a part of Afghanistan, appear either to have lived in complete independence, or, at most, in a state of loose connection with the Persian empire. For the Macedonians had here to contend with forces, of which only a small part was openly employed in the defense of Persia. On the other hand, they found them in a state of intimate union with the Indian princes. Here, also, Indian hired troops fought in the ranks, who, when they were overpowered by the Macedonians, fled for safety to Abisares, king of Cashmere. Princes of small states possessed elephants, few, indeed, in number, yet more than had been seen in the army of the great king. Alexander spared no pains to collect as many elephants as possible. If, indeed, he measured his military wants by the extravagant statements of Ctesias, he could not expect to cope with an Indian army in this species of armament, but he had now, without doubt, more accurate intelligence. Upon taking the town of Ora, the elephants of the Assaceni, thirty in number, fell into his hands. The Indian mercenaries abovementioned, when they fled to Abisares, let their elephants loose in the woods on this side the Indus, but Alexander succeeded, by means of the Indian hunters, whom he had brought with him, in catching and taming them afresh. Taxilas, a prince in modern Lahore, between the Indus and Hydaspes, (Vahuda) who, out of enmity towards his neighbor, declared himself for the conqueror, brought to him as he crossed the Indus, among other presents, thirty elephants. He thus collected a tolerable number, but they gave him no assistance in his war against Porus, because he could not transport them across the river in presence of the enemy. On the other hand, the hostile elephants made the passage uncommonly difficult: they stood in front on the opposite shore, and he was afraid to ship the horses lest they could not be made to land, or terrified at the sight and roaring of the elephants should leap from the floats into the water. It required all his boldness and practice in the art of war to effect a passage by night, amidst rain and storm, at a considerable distance from the camp of Porus. Hereupon followed the ever-memorable battle; everything considered, the most glorious victory which Alexander ever gained. In Persia he had to deal with hordes of barbarians, who, being brought together by the lash, were dispersed at the first resolute onset, with countless armies without an idea of tactics—with tribes who had become degenerate, the originally noble Persians through insolence, the lower ranks through slavery—with an effeminate despot, who always gave the first signal for flight, that his sacred person might run no danger. Here a different scene presented itself, an improved art of war, combined with the greatest personal bravery, a king, whose figure and size distinguished him as of heroic race, and was equaled by his undaunted courage; an army which might be conquered but not dishonored, for everyone, from the highest to the lowest, animated by the feeling of honor, were ready to offer up their lives in obedience to the ancient laws of the warrior caste. Porus was an Indian prince of subordinate rank: his territory lay in modern Lahore, on the left bank of the Hydaspes; the military force which so limited a territory was able to bring into the field, gives a high standard of Indian civilization at that time. In Porus's line of battle we recognize the war custom of the Indians, as represented in their heroic poems. The war chariots stood on the wings next the cavalry, in the middle was a row of 200 elephants at measured distances; behind them the infantry formed the second line, divided into separate bodies, which filled up the intervals, so that they could advance without hindrance, and the others retreat. These were the component parts of the Indian army: war chariots, cavalry, elephants, and infantry, from which it took the name of chaturangor or quadripartite. In the ancient world it seemed to be always most honorable to fight from a chariot. Thus the heroes of Homer; the far more ancient kings of Egypt, whom we still see with their magnificent team of horses: so also Arjunas, with his godlike attendant Krishnas, in the battle of the Kuru's and Pandu's; but Porus sat in radiant armor upon the hugest of his elephants, and, like the god Indras, launched from thence the lightnings of his javelins.

From want of acquaintance with the climate of India, (Ctesias had said that it never rained in India, but that the country was fertilized by the overflowings of the river,) Alexander, in making his campaign, had fallen upon the rainy months. Under other circumstances this might have proved his destruction, but was favorable to him in the battle. The war chariots stuck in the muddy ground, he outflanked the enemy with his numerous cavalry, and when at last the phalanx, after a stubborn and often doubtful contest with the elephants, pushed forwards, disorder and flight became general in the Indian army. The wounded king surrendered himself, when he found that all was lost: his two sons, and the whole of his officers, died upon the field. All the elephants of the conquered army fell into the hands of the victor, those at least which had not been slain in the action. Abisares, terrified at the fate of his ally, sent to Alexander a double tribute; together with seventy elephants, and Porus brought all that he had remaining. Thus was the power of Alexander increased in this department, though he was still far inferior to those whom he now intended to attack. It is well known how Alexander was compelled by the mutinous spirit of his troops to abandon his further designs. It remains a subject of doubt if he would have succeeded so well upon the Ganges as upon the Indus. According to the very credible statement of Diodorus Siculus (1. xvii. c. 93. —Plut. Alex. C. 02.) the Macedonians were alarmed by a report they had heard, that the king of the Gandarites and the Prasii kept on foot from four to six thousand elephants, with a proportionable army. When Alexander began his retreat by shipping down the Acesines and the Indus, he had two hundred elephants: besides these, he gained by conquest some others, at three different times, in the territories on the lower Indus: the number is not specified, it was probably not considerable: at the most he might have collected together three hundred. These he was at extraordinary pains to bring safe to the capital of his kingdom. They traveled down the left bank of the Indus as far as its delta. Afterwards, when Alexander made his painful march through the deserts of Gedrosia, in which his troops fell into the greatest difficulties by heat, thirst, and hunger, he sent them again upwards, on the right bank of the river, with the rest of his army, under the conduct of one of his most tried generals, Craterus, to lead them through the more inhabited road of Arachosia and Drangia. Craterus joined him again in Caramania. Doubtless the elephants served to adorn the ominous entrance of the conqueror into Babylon: they are mentioned there immediately after his death.

Alexander's vital powers were exhausted, perhaps, also, his good fortune, whilst his untamable spirit of adventure seemed to soar with untired vigor. It was not his fate to employ his new allies from the animal kingdom in the execution of his great designs: their images adorned his funeral car. The sarcophagus stood under an arched covering, upborne by pillars, upon which an acanthus was wreathed from the middle of the shaft into an Ionic capital; lions lay at the entrance, images of Victory stood at the four corners, the cell was latticed, all alike of gold. Paintings were disposed in the inner frieze under the bower of pillars: Alexander himself was represented sitting on a superb car, with his Macedonian and Persian bodyguards around; behind him a fleet; on one side squadrons of cavalry; on the other, elephants with their war trappings, their Indian leaders on their necks, and a Macedonian soldier on their backs. This was, doubtless, the first time that Grecian artists, and those of great distinction, were employed to portray foreign forms. From this we see what importance was attached to these living trophies of his Indian victories by those who were about Alexander. Sixty-four richly caparisoned sumpter-horses drew the car upon which this show was placed. Thus were the remains of the conqueror brought, with indescribable pomp, from Babylon to Alexandria, an object of wonder and admiration to the nations who were injured by his death as they had been by his life, although after-ages reaped great benefit from his deeds. From this time forth elephants have been employed for nearly three hundred years in endless wars undertaken for the dominion of the world, until the Romans at last remained victors upon the field of battle: first, by the successors of Alexander, in the different Satrapies, which were raised to independent kingdoms, in Macedonia, in Epirus, and afterwards by the Carthaginians and the princes of Western Africa; lastly, by the Romans.

---

1. The reader need hardly be reminded that, in what follows, Arrian's account has been adhered to, who, in everything that relates to Alexander's military history, is the only writer to be depended upon.

CHAPTER IV

FEBRUARY 1824

I KNOW NOT whence some of the moderns have taken up the opinion that the use of elephants has been of small importance, and only retained as a kind of oriental luxury. Is it from the speech which the rhetorician Quintus Curtius puts into the mouth of Alexander? This speech would have been in direct contradiction to the experience of his army and his own actions. Or was it from the bragging of the latter Romans, who might well talk when the danger was over, and they had only to look on in luxurious ease at the fights of animals in the circus? In critical times their opinion had been quite different, and after the experience of some victories which the elephants had gained over them, they took pains to get out of the way of these formidable animals. It is true that every weapon of offense must be judged of according to the entire circumstances of the military art in which it is employed. From his invincible dread of fire, the elephant has become, since the invention of gunpowder, unfit to be introduced into battle; but he is still the indispensable attendant of an army in Indian campaigns as a beast of burden, especially for the conveyance of heavy artillery. In the armaments and tactics of those times the elephants formed a sort of moving bulwark, behind which the troops could retreat or again sally forth. —They served for defence, and in turn required it to protect them from attack on the flank. If a column of heavy-armed infantry were formed in their front, they broke through the steadiest ranks, and then made fearful havoc amongst the flying bands. It became the custom to oppose to them light troops on foot or horseback, (provided that the horses were accustomed to their sight,) who followed them in every direction, took aim at their leaders with arrows or darts, and knew how to hit the vulnerable parts of the animal.

In speaking of the art of war, we must not neglect to take into consideration those things which work upon the imagination; whatever gives confidence to the soldier or strikes terror into the enemy becomes thereby advantageous, though otherwise unserviceable. With this view, in all ages, according to the diversity of manners and dress, military ornament has been employed, though of little use either for attack or defence. The effect which the elephants produced on their first appearance upon the imagination even of brave nations, the Greeks and Romans, was immeasurable; custom might deaden it in some degree, but it was never entirely lost. The Macedonians had learnt from the Indians to increase the impression of the massive size of the animal by showy trappings, and I am inclined to believe that they brought the elephants to the charge with a loud but measured music of drums and cymbals. The latter custom was universal in the movements of an Indian army, but so strange and striking to the Greeks that they could only explain it by reference to the imaginary campaign of Bacchus. When the soldiers of Eumenes, the troops of Antigonus, their arms glittering with gold, saw the elephants with purple canopies and towers coming down from the mountains over against them in the sunshine, they would not advance without their general, who was carried sick in an easy chair. (Plut. Eumeres, c. 14.) The towers are not to be understood literally: it is only a breast-work raised upon the sumpter saddle. In the ancients especially are to be found extravagant statements of the number of the soldiers which the elephants bore upon their backs. Reckoning by the weight, an elephant could always carry thirty men, as the burden of the strongest is estimated at from three to four thousand pounds. But how would these men have had room to turn themselves and use their arms? In this case, too, the elephants, through so unwieldy a burden, would have been unfit for all quick movements. In India the complement consisted of four men, one driver and three bowmen, to keep off the attacks on all sides. If the number was considerably above this, it must have been only for show.

The most important objection which has been made against the use of elephants is this, that they are of ambiguous utility, and may cause great mischief to those who employ them. For the elephants when wounded, deprived of their drivers and pressed backwards, often become unmanageable, turn against the troops in their rear, tread down the men, and throw the ranks into disorder. Against this danger, Hasdrubal, Hannibal's brother, contrived a certain but desperate remedy, by which the animals were sacrificed to prevent greater mischief. He armed the drivers with a chisel and hammer: when the elephant became so wild that all hope was lost of being able to govern him, a single smart blow upon the spine, where it joins the small, instantly put an end to his existence. (T. Liv. 1. xxvii, c. 48.) The art of the general consisted in driving the elephants into the thickest of the fray at the fortunate moment. By a judicious arrangement they might, whilst they covered a part of the front, contribute to the gaining of the battle without stirring from the place. It appears that the success was in most cases very decisive, or the contrary.

It would be entering into too wide a field to detail the war annals of the elephants throughout the whole range of ancient history. On the one hand, it is impossible to do this completely, because we have lost the original authors who treat of the events of so large a portion of this period; and on the other, it would lead to great prolixity, for it would be difficult to enumerate the battles in which elephants have been introduced. It will be enough to call the attention to some points of view which have not been sufficiently considered. The introduction of fresh elephants from India, and the ceasing of it, is intimately connected with the continuance of the relations which Alexander had formed with that country; from the more minute illustration of what has been told us respecting the African elephants, we shall perhaps obtain some results in natural history.

The war elephants of Alexander were naturally considered as hereditary possessions of the crown, and therefore we find them accompanying Perdiccas, who at first governed in the name of the Infant Successor, in his military expeditions. Immediately after the death of his heroic master, he terrified the refractory phalanx by bringing out his elephants against them, and used them to execute sentence of death upon the ringleaders of the sedition. (2. Curt. 1. X, c. 9.) —He led them into Egypt against Ptolemy, and wished to use them, as it seems, unadvisedly and without effect, in storming a fortress. In this campaign they passed the Nile twice. —(Diodor. Sic. 1. xviii, c. 34, 35.) After the violent death of Perdiccas, the next administrators and guardians of the realm remained in possession of the elephants: Antigonus, as their general, had thirty of them in Asia Minor; they assisted him to subdue Eumenes and Alcetas. When Polysperchon passed into Macedonia and Greece with the royal army, he took with him sixty-five elephants, which created a general alarm. (Diodor. Sic. 1. xviii, c. 70.) During the military anarchy which took place upon the death of Alexander the Great, adventurous and cunning generals violently appropriated to themselves not only the provinces, but the component parts of the armed force; and applied what was entrusted to them in the name of the nominal monarch, to from the groundwork of an independent power. These were the times of the Condottieri upon a large scale. —As upon the stage a few soldiers must sometimes represent the long train of an army, so the elephants appear to multiply themselves, being divided among different generals in countries widely remote. But they were, in reality, always the same; and for seven years after Alexander's decease, no other than those he had brought with him. It was only half a century after that they first began to use African elephants in war: in the meantime the custom of the Greek language had become established, of calling the driver of an elephant his Indian: this name was afterwards retained, though the driver might be an Ethiopian, a Mauritanian, or of any other country.

We have distinct information on what occasions in the first age after Alexander's death fresh elephants were brought from India, and even their number is mentioned. Eudamus had by treachery destroyed Porus, who, upon Alexander's death had been confirmed in his satrapy, and brought 120 of his elephants to Eumenes at Susa, (Ol. c. xv, 4.) and received for the expenses he had been at 200 talents. —(Diod. Sic. 1. xix, c. 14, 15.) The victories which Eumenes gained over Antigonus were of no use to him, because he was at last betrayed by his own army, and his whole power fell into the hands of the victor.

When Seleucus has established himself in the eastern provinces of the empire, from Babylon to Bactria, after an Indian campaign of which we do not know the details, he formed a league with Sandracottus, or rather with Chandraguptas, a powerful king and conqueror upon the Ganges, in which he employed Megasthenes as his ambassador. He took some provinces upon the borders of his realm from the Indian monarch, who sent against him 500 elephants. This must have happened before the battle at Ipsus. (Ol. cxix, 4.) The 400, or, according to others, 480 elephants, which are spoken of in the allied army opposed to Antigonus, belonged wholly to Seleucus. They performed essential services; for when Antigonus with his cavalry imprudently followed the flying enemy, they interposed themselves between him and his infantry, and cut off his retreat: the phalanx denuded of its cavalry surrendered, and Antigonus paid the forfeit of his life. —(Plut. Demetr. C. 85; and Athen. 1. vi, c. 78, both have it from Phylarchus.)

From this time Seleucus had a decisive superiority in this arm of war. —Demetrius listened with pleasure to his flatterers, when they turned into nicknames those things in which his rivals excelled him: they said he alone was the true king, Lysimachus the treasurer, Ptolemy the admiral, and Seleucus the king of the elephants. The command of the elephants was now, wherever they were employed, but particularly in Syria, an important office in the war department. To this an allusion is made in Terance, when the military prater boasts of having said in jest to the commander of the Indian elephants: "Is it this that makes thee so unruly, because thou art lord over the beast?" A celebrated author (Quatre mere de Quincy, p. 165, 166) refers this passage to the services of a Greek in the Persian army, and concludes thence, (as we have seen, contrary to history) that the Persian kings had elephants from time immemorial. But Terence had borrowed the part of the prater from Menander: the attic comedian, a contemporary of Demetrius and Seleucus, wrote his poems after the fashion of his age, and then there was no king in Persia. On the contrary, it may be supposed that Greece abounded in monsters who sought to make their fortunes in foreign war service. Under what king Thraso served is not expressly mentioned in the quoted scene; but it seems probable from the circumstances, that the king of Syria is meant, under whom the charge of the elephants was of the greatest importance. This is further confirmed, because the military prater of Plautus, the counterpart of Thraso, talks of having received a commission from Seleucus to raise recruits. (Plaut. Mil. Glorios. A. 1. Sc. 1.)

Nam rex Seleucus me opere rogavit maximo
Ut sibi latrones cogerem et conscriberem.

Amongst the lying deeds of Pyrgopolinices was this, that he had broken the thigh of an elephant in India with his fist. To make this boast have some historical probability, it can only be referred to the Indian campaign of Seleucus. That of Alexander was too remote an event.

With the exception of the Seleucidae, the other princes who had received elephants as heirlooms from Alexander had not an opportunity of increasing their number: their stock would gradually wear away, and at last altogether come to an end. The last kings of Macedonia had none left. Demetrius, as it appears, had saved a part of the elephants after the fall of his father Antigonus. He lost twenty to Pyrrhus, when he was driven out of Macedonia. With these Pyrrhus afterwards went to Italy, and this small number was sufficient to spread an inconceivable terror through the Roman army, and to effect its discomfiture. —These are the only Indian elephants which have ever been used in a campaign in Italy; it seems likely that they were either of that number which Alexander brought with him, or which Eudamus took for Porus. What a wonderful concatenation of events must it have required, that animals bred at the foot of the Himalayan mountains, after surviving so many violent revolutions of fortune, and being transferred with the scepter from one ambitious prince to another, almost half a century after the Indian campaign of Alexander the Great, in a remote region, in a different sphere of human existence, should fight against a nation who had not once heard their name, and in their boorish simplicity called them Lucanian oxen!

The average life of the elephant is reckoned at one hundred and thirty years. But this is to be understood of his condition as the domestic companion of man; for it is not easy to observe the age which he reaches in his wild state. The elephants which are kept singly here and there in the modern menageries of Europe, generally die after a short term of years. —But from this we can draw no conclusion with regard to the war elephants of the ancients. For, in the first place, they enjoyed a more southern climate: that of Syria might have been almost as favorable to them as their native land. Add to this, they were always kept in lively motion, they were kept in early exercise to prepare them for war. Besides, when an elephant is allowed sufficient room in a park to go about, he has no inclination for it, and becomes lazy and helpless. Lastly, the separation from others of his own kind must be very prejudicial to so sociable an animal. The war elephants, on the contrary, were exercised in troops to tactic evolutions and mock fights, and they were stimulated to exertion by emulation. The strongest and most courageous marched in front, the others followed, as the wild herds are wont. We are told by Pliny that when the Ajax of King Antiochus (for the names of Grecian heroes were given to these beasts, as they had before been named from the Indian mythology) had shown cowardice in passing a river, and as a punishment his rank had been taken away, and his silver harness given to Patroclus, the poor animal fretted himself to death. (Plin. Nat. Hist. 1. xviii, c. 5.) The free and sociable life of those elephants must have contributed to their cheerfulness and activity, as well as to their health. That those which were first captured lived to a tolerable age, appears in some measure from the campaigns of Pyrrhus; and further, that Antigonus Gonatus had still some remaining, and showed them to the ambassadors of the Gauls, to frighten them from their intended invasion.

I make the foregoing remark with reference to history. It is clearly made out that the kings of Syria have always had Indian elephants as long as they had any. And this continued towards 140 years after the battle at Ipsus. —The matter ended in a bloody and almost-tragical manner. When after the death of Antiochus Epiphanes the Syrian kingdom was administered in the name of the minor Antiochus Eupator, the Romans took a dishonorable advantage of this weakness of condition. They required the annihilation of the Syrian army; by order of their ambassador, Cn. Octavius, the ships of war were to be burnt, and the elephants put to death. A Laodicean, named Leptines, was so enraged at the horrible spectacle, that he killed Octavius. (Appian. Syriac. c. xlvi.)

We are very imperfectly acquainted with the history of the Seleucidae: we may be said to know only the foreside of it. Meantime I do not believe that we need to admit any other importations of elephants than those which are mentioned in historical books and fragments. I have spoken of those sent by Sandrocottus: this event took place, according to the most probable reckoning, a few years before the battle at Ipsus, and was, indeed, a most extraordinary circumstance. How powerful must a prince have been who could spare 500 elephants without materially weakening his force! It is ascertained upon good evidence that Antiochus kept up a friendly intercourse and correspondence by letter with the Indian King Amitrochates. (Athen. 1. xiv, c. 67.) By Antiochus we must here undoubtedly understand the first of his name, the son of Seleucus; and Amitrochates was a son and successor of Sandracottus. We are, alas, ignorant if more important political transactions took place between the two kings. Before the end of the reign of the next successor, arose the Parthian and Bactrian kingdoms, by which the connection with India was cut off, and the Syrian monarchy, which under its founder nearly corresponded with the extent of the Persian, was driven back far to the west. Antiochus the Great opened anew the road to the Indus, by his successful campaign against the Parthians and Bactrians. After gaining a battle against the Grecian king of Bactria, from political motives he entered into a league with him, acknowledged his independence, but caused him to deliver up his elephants. Hereupon he passed the Paropamisus, and renewed his friendship with the Indian king Sophagasenus, from whom he got so many elephants that the whole number amounted to 150. (Polyb. Hist. 1. xi, c. 32.) At the same time he possessed already above a hundred, which he used in the battle at Raphia against Ptolemaeus Philopator. These might have been the remainder of those belonging to Sandracottus, which 84 years before had helped to decide the battle at Ipsus. The command of the Romans to destroy the elephants of the King of Syria followed 40 years after the Bactrian campaign of Antiochus the Great, since which, no new supplies of these animals had taken place. That the Seleucidae considered this part of their armament as important, is evident from their coins, on which heads and whole figures of elephants appear in abundance.

We must now go back some space of time to make an observation upon the use of African elephants in war.—As neighbors, as rivals, and often as opponents of the powerful kingdom of Syria, the Ptolemies had motives sufficient not to be behind in any department of war. Indian elephants were not to be had, the thought therefore struck them of taming those from Ethiopia. But the Ptolemies were not masters of the country where they are indigenous; the rough inhabitants had, it appears, no idea of it, and it was scarcely to be hoped that regular supplies of them were to be got by treaties. The Kings of Egypt were therefore compelled to take upon themselves all the trouble of establishing themselves upon a strange territory, and of catching and breaking in the elephants by their own troops. This happened under the reign of Ptolemy Philadelphus: his general, Eunedes, sailed down the western shore of the Arabian Gulf, with a squadron, took possession, by surprise, of a small peninsula, entrenched it with ditch and mound, and then endeavored to gain over the inhabitants by friendly behavior. —The place was called Ptolemais, but distinguished from others of a similar name by the addition of its use and destination. Still further southward, near the mouth of the Arabian Gulf, close to the harbor of Saba, a second establishment was founded for the hunting of elephants. From these positions it was necessary to go a considerable way into the land, as far as the great rivers, to find the tracks of the elephants: the captured ones were then, without doubt, shipped to Egypt. It is observed, that the third Ptolemy, Euergetes, bestowed particular pains to break them in for war. But under his successor, the unpleasant discovery was made that all this pains was in some measure lost, because the Ethiopian elephants could not stand their ground against the Indian. For this cause the battle against Antiochus the Great, at Raphia, was on the point of being lost, the left wing of the Egyptian army having nearly fallen into confusion, but Ptolemy's generals gained the victory by other means.

In modern times, no elephant has been brought from Ethiopia, and still less been made the subject of accurate drawing or dissection. Upon the testimony of Ludolph, who was informed by his Abyssinian that the female elephants have no tusks, Cuvier supposes that the elephants of the eastern coast of Africa belong to the Indian species, and not to that of the western coast of Africa. Upon this point he appeals to the testimony of the ancients, but this is in direct opposition to him. Nothing can be more strong or pointed than the expressions of Polybius, in his description of the battle at

Raphia, (Polyb. 1. v. c. 84.) The Indian elephants were not only superior in strength to the Ethiopian, but the latter, from innate antipathy, could not come to the trial; they could not endure the voice and the smell of the Indian elephants, which is assuredly the strongest proof of an internal physiological difference. It is also, perhaps, treading upon the safest ground, to abide by the experience of the ancients, till more accurate observations of future travelers and naturalists gives room for scientific confirmation or refutation.

It is possible that in such a man of facts one or two may have escaped one, but I can call to mind no account of an engagement in which troops of Ethiopian elephants were opposed to those of Mauritania. The latter were first sued by the Carthaginians. They might have been induced thereto by the example of the Ptolemies, who, as possessors of Cyrene, were their neighbors; more probably, however, through their own experience in the Sicilian campaigns of Pyrrhus. In the earlier wars of the Carthaginians frequent mention is made of war chariots; these afterwards disappear, and the elephants seem to have taken their place. Five and twenty years after the first victory of Pyrrhus over the Romans, the Carthaginians, for the first time, and with brilliant success, made use of this newly acquired part of the art of war in the battle in which Regulus was made prisoner. Their general, Xanthippus, arranged his elephants upon the true principles of art, they broke through the columns of the infantry, and, in the literal sense, trod underfoot a great part of the Roman army, which was totally destroyed. The Roman soldiers became thereby so dispirited, that, for two years long, they durst not measure themselves in Sicily in the open field against Hasdrubal and his 140 elephants, till L. Caecilius Metellus gained the advantage over him. —This happened through the imprudent boldness of the elephant drivers, who wished to storm the Roman camp, by which the whole of the elephants fell a prey to the enemy. Metellus brought them to Rome, and employed day laborers to drive them through the circus with blunt spits, to inspire his countrymen with a sort of contempt towards the former objects of their fear.

The use of elephants was well suited to the political system of the Carthaginians, who were so anxious to spare their Phoenician population, and had recourse to stipendaries of all kinds. Of this sort were, to a certain degree, hired troops from the mountain of Atlas. When they suffered a loss in this quarter, it admitted of reparation, though not without expense and great establishments. They sent out their best generals with considerable detachments, to hunt the elephants, and the preparations for future campaigns was itself a campaign. Stables were made for the elephants upon the isthmus of the peninsula on which Carthage lay, and near them a spacious ground for their exercise. (Strab. 1. Xvii, p. 1189.) These animals performed distinguished services to the Carthaginians throughout the whole period of the three Punic wars, in Africa itself, in Sicily, in Spain and Italy; especially because the Carthaginians had to deal with opponents who could not employ the same weapon, otherwise they might have shared the fate of the Ptolemies. And the Carthaginian people entertained a grateful sense of their services; when the Romans issued the inhuman order that Carthage must be evacuated, and all was full of despair, the citizens called by name on their allies the elephants, which they had delivered up. (Plin. Hist. Nat. 1. viii. C. 5.) Cato the Censor thought it worthwhile, though in his annals he made no mention of the names of many generals, to record the name of one elephant, which had distinguished itself by its bravery in the Punic army. He was called Surus, and one of his tusks was broken off. (Plin. Hist. 1. viii. C. 5.) The Mauritanian elephants were also truly excellent, only good for nothing against the Indian. Where and how the trial was first made I cannot discover; but it seems to have been received as a well-known fact. In the battle against Antiochus the Great at Magnesia, the Roman commander, Domitius, kept his elephants, undoubtedly Mauritanian, in the rear, because he was convinced that if he should venture to oppose them in the field against the Indian elephants of Antiochus, they would do more harm than good.

From the Carthaginians the custom of using war elephants passed over to the Kings of Numidia and Mauritania. Jugurtha had some of them; —lastly Juba against Julius Caesar, and herewith the war history of the African elephants nearly comes to a conclusion.

The instances of the use of this weapon in the Roman armies are not very numerous; we have seen one. Flaminius also led elephants against King Philippus of Macedonia. The question naturally occurs why the Romans did not introduce into their armies in a permanent manner a weapon which had been so often used with effect against themselves, after they became masters of the northwest of Africa? —That the Roman soldiers made little account of such opponents, as has latterly been maintained, is altogether an unfounded supposition. When Caesar's veteran army found that L. Scipio and Juba had altogether ninety elephants, it fell into great consternation, because this sort of fighting was somewhat unusual. Meantime Juba was called away by another enemy, and Scipio retained only the thirty which belonged to him. The fifth legion again took courage, and requested to be placed opposite the elephants. When the victory was gained, they got for their reward the image of the animal for their standard.

There are other causes by which the use of elephants became not indispensable to the Romans, or rather in some measure impracticable. When they had destroyed all the kingdoms founded upon Alexander's conquests, there remained in the east no enemies to conquer, except the Parthians, and against the Tartar mode of warfare of these people so ponderous a weapon could not be employed. Besides, they would have had trouble enough to maintain, and especially to provide with water the elephants in the burning sandy deserts, where they had to follow the Parthians. The other warlike boundary of the Romans was the Rhine and the Danube; in that rough climate in the morasses and forests, a southern animal, so sensible of cold, could never be brought to exist for any length of time. Perhaps also a moral cause might cooperate, the Roman leaders might not wish that their soldiers in the field of battle should fight behind a kind of bulwark and depend upon extrinsic aid.

However that might be, after the latter ages of the republic, the Romans used the Mauritanian elephants only for the show fights of the circus, and they destroyed them in such a manner that no remnant was left. For I cannot help considering this as the only cause of the destruction of the breed in the countries about Mount Atlas, whither, on account of the intervening deserts, no new herds could wander from the Senegal and the Niger. Buffon assets, but without the authority of history, that the increase of population has driven out of these countries an animal which requires large room. In the flourishing times of the Roman empire, till the Antonines, the province of Africa was much more thickly peopled, and better cultivated than it has ever been since; and yet in the third century of our Christian era there were elephants there.[1] In the time of Caesar, indeed, their number may have been very much diminished, because the Carthaginians, and the Numidian and Mauritanian princes, had hunted them for 200 years. Meantime war was not nearly so murderous to the breed as the circus: in the intervals of peace, the tamed animal was carefully attended to, and many a campaign passed over without the loss of a single beast. In the show fights, on the contrary, the life of the animal was wantonly sacrificed; the exhibition was thought wanting in pomp, if no blood was shed; this horrid carnage was renewed yearly, and was not confined to Rome alone; the capitals of the provinces had also their combats of animals. No time was left to exhausted nature to recruit itself. Among the numerous modes of Roman luxury, this madness was not the least. Interchanged with elephants, lions, tigers, panthers, hyenas, appeared upon the arena. Africa, so fertile in wild beasts, was almost exhausted, and if this had continued long at the same rate, the Romans would have remained the only beasts of prey upon the face of the earth. Unheard-of labor and sums of money wee expended to corrupt still more the minds of an idle and cowardly populace by this barbarous diversion. At times, however, the voice of humanity was heard; the people took part with the elephants against Pompey the Great, and loaded him with execrations on the festival which he himself gave.

Unfruitful indeed for science, because there was no Aristotle to observe, but a more harmless gratification of curiosity it was, when the emperors procured from far distant countries peaceful animals, as the giraffe, the zebra, and others, and only led them in procession as a show, or tried by all sorts of tricks to exhibit in a striking light the dexterity of the animals. From this we discover at least, that the Mauritanian elephants were not behind the Indian in docility. They were taught to trace Greek letters with the trunk, to climb up and return upon ropes stretched obliquely, though what sort of ropes must they have been? Four carried in a litter a fifth, as if in the pangs of labor. The elephants of Germanicus, who succeeded in the attempt to transplant them into Italy in the tame state, executed a dance, not only in measure, but with movements according with the character of the music arranged in pairs, dressed out in ornaments after the difference of the male and female sex, they laid themselves down on pillows and carpets beside a table pompously set out, and ate their meal in due order from golden and silver cups and plates, as we are assured, with all the observances of good breeding and respect. —We may easily conceive how such a grotesque show would delight the gaping crowd, who were wont to be drawn away, as the satirical poet says, from the most refined dramatic representations by the sight of a white elephant.

Sive elephas albus vulgi converteret ora. [HORACE.]

White elephants could only come from India, (probably by sea from Alexandria,) and indeed from the further peninsula: at least I do not remember that this variety has been spoken of elsewhere. Could the undertaker's love of gain, who must always excite the wonder of the populace by something new, have carried him so far? —or did the ambassadors of the Seres and India bring such honorary presents to Augustus? Generally speaking, Mauritania supplied the circus with elephants: the emperors sent thither their own officers upon hunting excursions. (Aelian. 1. x. c. 1.). That Ethiopia was not sufficiently accessible to the Romans for this purpose, may be concluded from the campaign of discovery under Nero, which has been already mentioned.

---

1. Upon a coin of Gordianus is to be seen the amphitheatre, and in it the combat of an elephant and a bull, with the inscription, Munificentiâ Gordiani Aug.

CHAPTER V

APRIL 1824

SINCE THE time of Aristotle, the ancients have done little or nothing for the physiology of animals; but what they tell us of the manners and capacity of the animals which they were acquainted with from personal observation, deserves to be thoroughly investigated. This is especially the case with their stories of elephants. Here they had experience in abundance, on account of the manifold uses of the elephant in war, and the games of the circus. Through the intercourse of men with beasts, their individuality becomes unfolded, while in a state of nature they seem to have only a character belonging to the genus, and the extraordinary qualities which may become observable among a great number of cases, is not to be directly rejected. The European naturalist, who is only acquainted with elephants singly, and has observed them in a state of wretched captivity, is not particularly justified in combating the evidence of the ancients in this particular.

But besides the written testimony, there is another kind which has reached us from antiquity, I mean the representations of the plastic art. May I be allowed to call the attention of naturalists to this point. Zoology has probably many yet unnoticed points of contact with archaeology: a particular interest was attached to the object in question, because we are not yet fully acquainted with the divisions of the species, and because the ancients have delineated elephants from countries, from which either none have come to the modern naturalist, or no more can come. So soon as we know the origin of an ancient carving, we can say in what country the elephant represented upon it was native. In Greece and Asia Minor, since the time of Alexander the Great, no other elephant but the Indian was seen; in Egypt, under the Ptolemies, none but the Ethiopian; and in Rome, in the time of the Emperors, only the Mauritanian. I will not assert that every time new studies were made after nature; but the artist imitated known works of art, or the shape of the animal so frequently seen played before his imagination, and necessarily with the individual character of the species belonging to a particular country. This would only then be deviated from when the form should have been portrayed quite arbitrarily, or after a manner settled by agreement. —But with the ancient artists, who bestowed so much pains upon various tribes of animals, many of them, too, very unfavorable for sculpture, and who possessed so keen a perception of animal physiognomy, this consideration was chiefly to be attended to, when the figure is introduced as subordinate, as, for instance, in the bas reliefs of the bacchanal processions. Here the proportion of its real size to the human figures is sacrificed to the symmetry of the whole: it belongs, also, to the conventional mode of representation, when the whole body is covered with oblique crossing lines, as with a network, to represent the wrinkles and folds in the skin of the elephant, which yet have their anatomical meaning. —But the artist certainly worked after nature when the colossal animal appeared as the principal object upon a monument. Such large works served as a pattern in small to the sinker of a die for coins. I have already spoken of the coins of the Seleucidae. Elephants likewise often appear upon the Roman coins, sometimes single, sometimes yoked together in bigae or quadrigae. Julius Caesar introduced an elephant upon his coins. Strange explanations have been thought of: it was a symbol of the conquest of Africa, as on other coins of the first emperor, a crocodile denotes the subjection of Egypt. Under the following emperors, the single elephant betokens extraordinary festivals of the circus; the inscription *"Munifi-cencia Aug,"* points it out distinctly. The Romans did really sometimes yoke elephants to their chariots: first Pompey, at his African triumph, but it was found that the gate was too small to admit their entrance. The quadrigae with elephants upon the imperial coins are, however, not so much referred to triumphs of that kind, as to the public monuments, where the statues of the emperors were placed upon quadrigae. This is the more certain, because the coins show also triumphal arches with two elephant chariots on the elephants on the upper surface. The elephant also was frequently represented in Rome, in full size, in brass and marble; and here the artist could never be in ant of living models. It is, therefore, to be wished, that the Roman coins on which elephants are impressed (the originals are here to be understood, and in well preserved specimens; for in so nice a point of difference, copperplates are not to be relied on) were examined with an experienced zoological eye, and compared with larger works of ancient art. By means of this, one might discover if the Mauritanian elephant in its entire structure resembled that of Southern Africa, or whether it has not a peculiar specific character, agreeing neither with the elephant of Southern Africa nor with the Indian, and belonged to a third kind, now extinct. —It seems hazarding too much to assert that what is uniformly presented to the eye on these coins, and I can observe such on a few originals which lie before me, for instance, a higher make of the legs, the back not hanging obliquely against the thigh, the large flaps of the ears—it were surely hazardous to say that these peculiarities are mere mistakes of the draughtsman. We are, it is true, very scantily provided with drawings of African elephants in the zoological works of the moderns. One single one, and that a very moderate one, is to be found in the essay of Perrault. This elephant was from Congo, and presented to Lewis 14th by a king of Portugal. The woodcut in Gesner's book of animals, in which are so many characteristic figures deserving commendation, seems, if one may judge by the large ear-flaps, to represent an African elephant, but does not look like any created thing; and the publisher would have done well to add the remark, as with the drawing of the urns: "This is not the real likeness, and must not be mistaken for an exact copy." We have many drawings of the Indian elephant, though few very correct. The best are those in the folio edition of the often-mentioned royal French menagerie; the female elephant, in passionate movement, is masterly. How much it is to be wished that competent artists would dedicate their talents to zoology! If the drawing of an animal is liable to objections, as a work of art, it can seldom satisfy the zoologist.

After the age of Julius Caesar the Roman history is silent about elephants for some centuries. Didius Julianus, when he expected the attack of his rival, in his extreme necessity made a weak attempt to break in for war the elephants then kept in Rome for pomp and festivals, and, except on this occasion, the Roman emperors never employed them. The kings of the Parthians also had no war elephants, but in the later Persian Empire they again make their appearance; and in the wars against the Sassanidae the Roman and Byzantine armies had often to contend against troops of them. That the Persian monarchs of that dynasty have constantly kept them on foot is an ascertained fact, and we have no need to appeal upon this point to the doubtful respectability of the Persian historians. It is authenticated by eyewitnesses, both of the fourth and the sixth century of our ear, by Ammianus Marcellinus and Procopius. —In speaking of the numbers, it is probable that great exaggerations have crept in, sometimes on the part of the Roman, oftener of the oriental historians. Gibbon has very properly thrown suspicion upon the 700 elephants in the army of the first Sassanides, Artaxerxes, together with the pretended victory of Alexander Severus.[1] Twelve hundred elephants are ascribed to Kosru Parviz, or Cosroes the Second: naturally enough in consequence of the Indian conquests of Mishirvan.

The Persian historians state that this monarch, by means of his generals (for he did not once give himself the trouble to take the field) conquered India as if by a coup de main: and that his army advanced even as far as Serendib, i.e. to the island of Ceylon. —(Silvestre de Sacy Antiquites de la Perse. Traduction de l'histoire de Mirkhond). The last, however, even for an oriental figure of rhetoric, is too strong an hyperbole, and I confess I think it may be classed with the assertion of Mirkhond, that Ardeshir, the founder of the dynasty, subjected all the provinces of the earth to his scepter. When Nushirvan had in this manner made himself master of all India, he found it expedient to give it up again, and to satisfy himself with a province upon the borders: a prudent foresight on the part of the historian to prevent enquiries as to what had become of these conquests. The truth is, that the Sassanidae had never, any more than the Achaemenidae, ruled over any part of the countries beyond the Indus. In my opinion, we bestow all possible honor upon that dynasty, when we allow that their empire, in the height of its greatness, comprehended Cabul and Afghanistan. The Sassanidae might procure their war elephants in the same manner as the Seleucidae, who were at first real kings of Persia: namely, by stipulation with the neighboring Indian chiefs of the northern

Peninsula. The numbers must, in all probability, from this consideration be much reduced. It has been shown that, during this period, especially in the latter half of it, a very brisk intercourse took place between Persia and India; and, even according to the Persian accounts, India always appears in a state of superior cultivation in science, art, and commercial industry; always imparting, never receiving. This deserves a separate discussion, which I will not here forestall. Among the literary treasures communicated in the time of Nushirvan, only one circumstance is recorded, the journey of his physician Barzuyeh, and the translation of the Hitopadesa. I am also convinced, that upon further examination much will be discovered which has hitherto passed for original in Persic and Arabic, but was in reality brought at that time from India, and through the Persic and the Pehloi language has spread itself into other languages and other countries.

I have also asserted, in the beginning of this dissertation, that the native tribes of Africa have never been able to tame and break in the elephant. Not to suppress anything which may be alleged to the contrary, I think it proper to cite a later mention of the use of war elephants in Abyssinia, which is to be found in a book where one would not expect to find it, I mean the Koran. Abrahah, minister of the Emperor of Abyssinia, in Arabia Felix, is said to have made an expedition against Mecca, in the very year of Mahomed's birth, to lay waste the Kaaba. We are assured that he had elephants in his army. That upon which Abrahah rode, as soon as he saw the holy city, took fright and ran away, and the rest followed him. Hereupon a flock of wonderful birds overwhelmed the flying soldiers of Abrahah in a body, with stones which they threw down. —So the commentators explain the dark text of the Koran in the hundred and fifth section, or the Surat Alfil. Had this custom then remained in Upper Ethiopia from the times of the Ptolemies? Or, had the

Sassanidae, during their Arabian wars, learnt the use of the elephants from the Abyssinians? Or, did they acquire it by means of an immediate communication with India? Or, lastly, has the prophet only dreamt the miracle in one of his confused visions? We must leave this to be made out by those who are learned in the Arabian and Abyssinian languages and history. Be that as it may, the above mentioned position, that the Aborigines of Africa have, from time immemorial, only slain the elephant and fed upon its flesh, and not been able to tame them without foreign assistance, is by no means impugned thereby. Besides, the Abyssinians are of Arabian extraction, and have only lately wandered into their present settlements. I shall afterwards remark a trace in the Abyssinian language which, in this respect, carries us directly to India.

Hitherto I have endeavored to collect and compare the testimonies of the ancients concerning the object of this treatise, with continual reference to India, the country of our researches, to its position in respect to hither Asia, and the whole of the western world, its internal condition, and outward relation. I will now lay before the reader some considerations drawn from the language, the mythology and poetry, which may be important either in regard to the modes of thinking and manners of the inhabitants, or may serve to paint with livelier traits some particulars in the natural history of the animal.

In the first place, the names of the elephant, in the Sanskrit they are very numerous, as would naturally happen in an object which is presented to the view in daily life, and in the most manifold relations, to which, at the same time, on account of its great and extraordinary qualities, poetry can never renounce its pretensions.

I will not make a complete enumeration of its names, but only distinguish those which deserve notice for their obvious signification, or which by their resemblance to other languages can lead us into an etymological track.

From its proboscis the elephant is called *hastin, karin,* from hasta, kara, the hand. The comparison is very obvious, and Aristotle has already made it; the Latins call the trunk manus, as well as the Indians.

The particular manner in which the elephant drinks, by taking the water first into his trunk and afterwards pouring it down his throat, is indicated with the greatest brevity by the names dvipa, *twice drinking,* anekapa, *more than once drinking.*

From its projecting tusks, the elephant has got the name of *dantin,* corresponding to the Latin *dentatus,* to the French *dentu,* from *danta,* a tooth; of *dvirada,* the *double-toothed,* from *rada,* a tooth; the root is rad, *rodere.* It is also called *kunjara,* from *kunja,* which particularly signifies an elephant's tooth. As all elephants have not tusks, but as they are an indispensable weapon for those employed in war, so the names derived from them are often supplied by others. The word *naga* is strangely enough used to signify both a serpent and an elephant. I know not whether the essential reason is a comparison of the "lithe proboscis," with the body of the snake, or that both creatures bear this name because their dwelling is in the forests of the mountains. *Nàga* may be a patronymic derivative from naga by a lengthening of the first vowel. I rather incline to the latter opinion, because *nagaja* signifies the creature of the mountain.

Why they have also given to the elephant the name of Lotus flower, *padma,* I have not been able to discover.

In common life *gaja* appears to have been the most usual denomination, which has passed into more recent dialects with some variation of the pronunciation.

As the elephant is only native in India, one might naturally suppose that the name would travel together with the thing itself into the countries of the west. This, however, does not hold good, as far as concerns the Greek language. The word 'elephas,' as we have already seen, at first signified ivory, and was, probably by means of Grecian travelers on the western coast of North Africa, transferred to the animal itself, before anything was known of Indian elephants. The poverty, in this point, of a language otherwise so rich, might produce misconception. Pausanias takes refuge in circumlocution. (Pausan. A.H. c. xii, 4.) Pliny very gravely assures us that the captured elephants are soon tamed by a drink made from barley, while the Greek author whom he followed only meant to say that ivory might, in some degree, be softened by an infusion of barley. (Plin. Hist. Nat. 1. viii, c. 7. Capti celerriimè mitificantur hordei succo. Compare Quatre-mère de Quincy Jupiter Olypian, p. 419.)

Many derivations have been attempted of the word 'ελεφας,' but none of them can be considered as satisfactory. In my opinion, there are two considerations which ought never to be lost sight of, the one is the original Homeric signification, the other, that we are not to give an account of the nominative, which has been mutilated by throwing out two letters, but of the entire word, which appears in the other cases, ΕΛΕΦΑΝΤος.

In the glossaries of the Zend and the Peloi, which we msut now have recourse to for assistance, I find in the first language no name at all, and in the second such as are not allied to anything that I am acquainted with. Peloi, *Banbarita*, elephant; *Zangrotu*, raging elephant. On the contrary, the Persian name *pil* is widely diffused in the Aramaic languages of western Asia. I leave it to those who are acquainted with these languages to find out by what series of changes this word has passed from one of them into the other, and where it seems to be originally native. I would only observe, that it is also to be found in the Sanskrit, and that in a fuller form, *pilu*. The composer of the

Amara-Kosha has, indeed, omitted this name in his chapter upon the elephant, but quoted it among the words which admit of various significations. Besides this, *pilu* signifies a particular kind of tree, and an arrow, this last agreeing with the Latin *pilum*, the Swedish *pil*, etc. In the supplemental lexicon *Tricanda*-Sêsha, this name of the elephant is brought up, together with several others. Likewise, in the *Medini*, an alphabetical lexicon of synonymes, and in the Harabali, a catalogue of uncommon expressions. —The classical meaning of the word in Sanskrit is also sufficiently ascertained. I do not remember ever to have met with it in reading Indian books, and cannot, therefore, state in what sort of writings and how old it is used. Neither do I know from whence the Indian grammarians derive it; —from its form I suppose it may be reckoned amongst those words which are formed by the Unâdi-Afixes. In the meantime, it seems to me that the bare existence of this word in the Sanskrit must give a new turn to etymological researches. The wishing to introduce foreign words into India for this object, would be carrying wood to the forest. And since the word *pil* nowhere occurs in the Hebrew text of the Old Testament, but first appears in the Chaldaic and Syrian paraphrases, and, further, since it stands single in the Arabic, as I am assured by a learned Orientalist, it has most probably come into Persia with the elephant drivers, and from thence been transplanted into the Aramaic languages.

If indeed, we could depend upon the heretofore quoted signification of the word Philae, we should have a far older trace of foreign derivation. In this, the Coptic gives us no assistance; for the Coptic names of the elephant, ΕΛΦΙΝΟΣ and ΔΕΛΦΙΝΟΣ, which I find stated in Kircher, appear to have originated from the corruption of the Greek. If it could ever be proved that the elephant was named *phil* in the old Egyptian, this would be a fact of no small moment in establishing the probability of an intercourse between Egypt and India before the times of authentic history.

This word, then, has, through the intervention of the Arabic, found its way into some European languages. —Ivory is called in Spanish mar*fil*, in Portuguese mar*fim*; the bishop at chess in Spanish *alfil* (pure Arabic with the article), or, by a corrupted pronunciation, *arfil*. It is well known, that, among the four members of an Indian army, the pieces which we call bishops represent the elephants, the towers or rooks, the war chariots.

If the word *fil* were native in Arabic, one might expect to find it again in the language of the Abyssinians. —But the name of the elephant in Ethiopic is nage, altogether Indian. This seems to indicate a communication, but in what age it may have happened, I dare not undertake to decide.

The Latin name *barrus* is unquestionably of African extraction, perhaps Punic, for, in the Mauritanian language, the elephant was called *Caesar*. The name of ivory, *eubr*, proves that the Italian tribes did not first become acquainted with this article of merchandise through the Greeks—to me, however, it is altogether inexplicable.

In the Amara-Kosha the elephant is not treated of with beasts of burden, the ox, the camel, etc. but in the chapter on war, together with and before the horse. We must not here pass over in silence how in the same book the proportion of the component parts of an army is first. One elephant, one war chariot, three horsemen, five infantrymen: these ten parts make up a set: 2,187 such sets a full army: this taken tenfold is a great army, called akshauhini. The grammarian has doubtless taken this account from theoretical writings on the art of war. The whole is founded upon the numbers 4, 10, 3, 7. The members of the army are four: the single parts in one set are ten; and the number of the required sets is the seventh power of three. It is sufficiently understood that it never was in reality so considered, but it is remarkable enough that the arrangement was made upon arithmetical principles. In relation to the other component parts the number of the elephants seems to be reckoned too high, according to the historical and even the mythological examples. But we must remember that four men were required for each elephant, and at least ten for each war chariot, and also that in a great army 306,150 stood in battle array.

I nowhere find a tradition or mythological proverb of the first taming of the elephant. It is with this as with all the institutes of Indian civilization; they are everywhere supposed, and reach beyond the memory of man. The Persian proverb makes a boastful fable upon this point, because it has no real pretensions; the proverb of the Indians is silent in the security of possession. The animal appears a companion of the Gods as well as of men, for Indras, the monarch of the firmament, rides upon an elephant; he is, too, a willing beast of burden, even in reference to cosmogony, as the four cardinal points are supported by elephants placed under them.

How highly the Indians have always valued the intellectual capacities of this animal sufficiently appears from one mythological symbol: Ganesas, the God of all science and inventive art, is represented with an elephant's head. The organic conditions, without which reason, or anything like reason, cannot unfold itself, are to be found in the elephant. In his trunk he has an instrument of various and arbitrary motion, endued with a fine sense of touch, of which most animals are altogether destitute: and this hand is at the same time the conducting organ for the sensations of smell, the sense to which properly belongs the discrimination of the internal chemical characters of things. The feats of activity which the elephant performs excite the more wonder on account of his massive structure and apparent helplessness. Just so was the science of the primitive world, struggling up against the load of the world of sense; yet with inimitable self-possession and gentleness, and even with a certain wiliness, seizing upon and disentangling the incorporeal truth.

Against the symbol as such there is nothing to object; but when visibly portrayed, it must always appear a horrible monstrosity. Upon general principles it is easy to perceive that a beast's head, be it what it may, must always be revolting upon a human body. Everything in the human form bespeaks humanity, but above all the countenance in an infinitely high degree; and when expectation is here disappointed, and where mind and genius should beam from the brow, nothing meets the eye but the dull and gloomy expression of bestiality, we feel ourselves shocked and offended. On the other hand, some human limbs must be associated with the face to smooth the transition to the bestial form. This has been observed by the Egyptian artists in their sphinxes, and by the Grecians in their centaurs, tritons, etc. according to the finest perceptions of natural taste. —Grecian art has exhausted in all its gradations the mystery of creating beautiful monsters, in which the physiological contradiction is disguised by the physiognomical harmony: only when the mythological character was too strictly defined, it was compelled to make a minotaur or a hebon, forms to which the eye can never reconcile itself. In Greece, art, after a long struggle, at last freed itself from the guardianship of the priests, as poetry had done at an earlier period. Before that, the idols of the Greeks had no better an appearance than those of other nations: they adored a Ceres with a horse's head, and in an age of the highest cultivation, Diana of Ephesus remained a priestly monster. Among the Egyptians the symbol was portrayed without restriction, and hence the innumerable heads of hawks, ibises, crocodiles, lions, rams, jackals, and dogs on human bodies. Ganesas, on the contrary, stands almost unique in his kind: the imagination of the Indians has employed itself more in varying the human limbs. When, therefore, in the Indian idols some new scandal has been announced as a thing unheard of, it seems as if the polytheism of all antiquity was forgotten.

The monstrosity of Ganesas is perhaps softened by an imitation of nature, which has something naïf and droll. The elephant loves to grasp tufts of branches and leaves with the end of his trunk to drive off the flies: in like manner Ganesas stands reverently before his father, as the servants of the great are wont to do, and brandishes, with uplifted proboscis, the costly fly-lash, the chamaram. —Or he sits with a little open box of sweetmeats in his hand, and with great gravity takes something out, as the elephant also is known to be fond of such dainties.

---

1. Gibbon Hist. etc. ch. viii, note 49. —Gibbon, however, goes much too far, when he asserts that elephants have never been employed in such large numbers either in India itself or elsewhere. The deeply read, or to speak more accurately, the elegantly read historian, when he made the remark, forgot Sandracottus, the battle at Ipsus, and many other things, which are as well authenticated as if they had happened only yesterday. What can the accounts which recent travellers give us of the decayed power of the Great Mogul, and of the war establishment of the modern Indian princes, when the use of fire-arms has made elephants almost useless, what information can they give us of those nuclear times, of which Pliny says, elephant magnâ exparte orients bella conficiunt? Plutarch (Alex. C. 62) makes the striking remark, that the statement of the six thousand elephants of the King of the Prasians and the Gandaritae is certainly not exaggerated; one thing clearly results from it, that not long afterwards Sandracottus resigned 500 to Seleucus.

CHAPTER VI

MAY 1824

F ROM THE doctrine of the transmigration of souls, we may estimate the moral rank which the Indian philosophers assigned to the elephant among animals. The bodies and forms into which the soul enters in a new life, are determined according to the property or principle of action which has been predominant during the earthly life of a man. Of these principles there are three: real essence, or the true and good; passion; and darkness, i.e. sensual identity. The transmigrations of those, with whom the first was the ruling principle, are actual transfigurations or true apotheoses: the souls of the second order also reenter only into human or superhuman forms; the imprisonment in animal bodies is reserved for those only who have given themselves up to the quality of darkness. —And here again there are three gradations; to the lowest belongs the transmigration into mineral and vegetable substances, into all kinds of worms, fishes, snakes, amphibia, tame cattle, and among the ignoble beasts of prey, the jackal. It is farther ordained in the laws of Menu, or Manus; "elephants, horses, men of the servile race and barbarians (Mlêcha's), lions, tigers, and boars, are the middle conditions, to which the quality of darkness leads." In the highest gradation of this order there are no animal transmigrations, except into birds. The speculations to which this doctrine may lead belong not to our present purpose. But with respect to the arrangement in the above-mentioned award, I should think the most material circumstance is brought forward to view, namely, that the elephant, and, after him, the horse, are announced as the noblest among quadrupeds. Besides, in the Sanskrit, the names of the lion, tiger, elephant, ox, attached to another word, are of equal import, and are used to denote the preeminence among any order of beings.

Among the accounts which the ancients have handed down to us concerning the elephant, the most wonderful and incredible of all is, that it has a sort of religion. In the Mauritanian mountains, Pliny tells us, probably upon the authority of Juba, the herds of elephants, upon the appearance of the new moon, march down to a river called Amilo, there they purify themselves with a solemn sprinkling of water, and, after saluting the star, they return back into their forests. Whatever ridicule may be cast upon the ancients for their credulity in this point, I cannot forbear to think it worthy of remark, that this Mauritanian tradition of the reverence which the elephants pay to the moon, appears likewise to have been current in India. A fable of the Hitopadesa indisputably refers to it, and in spite of the fantastic freedom of the composition, the poetic tales in this book are always founded upon generally received opinions concerning the beasts. I insert the whole fable exactly according to the original. To understand it properly, it is necessary to be informed that, among other names, the moon is called Sasin, a possessive derivative from sasa, the hare: and also Sasânka, from the same word, and anka, a spot or mole, because in the spots of the moon's disk the form of this animal may be traced. Chandras, the god of the moon, sometimes bears a hare, or carries its image upon his standard.

IN DEALING WITH MIGHTY KINDS, it is often the part of prudence to make use of specious pretexts: by the pretext of the hare in the moon, the hares prolonged their existence.

How was that, said I? The birds told me the
following tale.

Once upon a time, when there was a want of rain in the rainy season, a herd of elephants, parched with thirst, said to their leader, Master! How shall we contrive to live? Have not the small animals a well-watered habitation? And we for want of water wander about like blind creatures? What shall we do? Hereupon the king of the elephants went forward a little way, and showed them a pure lake. Meantime the hares which dwelt upon its banks were crushed underfoot by the herd of elephants. A hare, whose name was Worm-face, thereupon bethought himself; this herd of elephants, urged by the desire to drink, will come back every day, and then our whole race must perish. Thereupon, an old hare, called Victor, said, "Let us not lose heart. I will find means to defend you against them."—With this promise he went forward, and while he was going on, he considered with himself: "What shall I say when I meet the herd of elephants.—For they say, 'with his touch the elephant, with their breath snakes destroy. The ruler of the land in protecting, villains with smiles decoy.' I will get upon the top of a mountain, and make myself known to the leader of the herd." As he spoke this, the leader of the herd said to him, "Who art thou, and whence?" He answered, "I am an ambassador, sent from the sacred moon." The leader of the herd replied, "Speak thy business."

Victor spake.

When swords are drawn, the ambassador holds his peace:

to prevent war he speaks boldly what he ought to speak. Now I speak by her command: Hear! These hares are the protégées of the moon, thou hast not well done to drive them away. Because they are my protégés, I hear the standard of the hare. When the ambassador had so spoken, the leader of the herd was startled, and said, what has been done was done unwittingly; hereafter I will not come back again. The ambassador spake: Then make thy obeisance to the sacred moon, who here trembles in the lake for anger, appease her and depart. Thereupon he led him thither the same night, showed him the trembling image of the moon in the lake, and commanded the elephant to bow himself down. —"Godlike Lord! What thou hast done unwittingly will be forgiven thee!"—Hereupon the hare dismissed the leader of the elephants. Therefore say I, "It is prudent to make use of pretexts and so forth."

Here the elephant suffers himself to be good-humoredly outwitted: so also in the fable with the jackal, who decoys him into a morass. It is not to be wondered at, if in the Hitopadesa, in which there predominates a playful view of the animal world, the intellectual powers of the elephant are undervalued, as in the following proverb:—

"Prudence is mightier than strength, through the want of which elephants have fallen in such servitude. This lesson is taught by the hand drum of the elephant driver and its clatter."

The idea is here stated partially in a satirical manner. It is true that the elephant loses his freedom at first through superior cunning: but if he were not susceptible of an unconquerable sympathy for man, it would be a hard matter to educate him to a serviceable subordination.

In other parts of the book much is said in his praise.

His free spirit:

"Lions, men, and also elephants, wander far from home:

but crows, cowards, and timorous animals stay there till death."

His sympathy for his fellow creatures:

"The good are always willing to help the good:

"The elephant bears the burden for his brethren, who sink into the morass."

His strength:

"A stronger must be combated! —He who says so, does not think it."

"To engage with an elephant, would soon bring a man to death."

Among the savage inhabitants of the forest, the lion, of whom so much mention is made in the old poets, though the modern travelers in India say nothing of him, is considered as superior to the elephant. It is only in the latter that he finds a worthy opponent. "The lion, it says, lets the jackal go, even when he approaches close to him, and slays the elephant." The combats of the most powerful natures are finely portrayed in the following lines.

"What is a home or a foreign abode to the prudent brave? Into whatever country he goes, he subdues it by the majesty of his arm. In whatever forest the tooth-claw-tail-armed lions may wander, even in that he slakes his thirst with the blood of the chief of the elephants."

According to this idea are formed the two stone elephants, which stand before one of the temple grottoes of Ellore, and roaring tear in pieces an elephant under their paws. It is true, that, with a liberty easily granted to sculpture, the proportion of size in these groups is reversed even if the elephant is supposed to be a young one. The copper plates which we have, do not allow us to judge of the style; the idea is grand, and the object worthy of the most exalted efforts of art. But according to a proverbially popular expression, this victory over his mighty opponent only tends to the lion's death, perhaps because he surfeits himself with his blood. A beautiful saying in the Hitopadesa refers to this:

"Foes soon destroy a kingdom, which is a vessel of sins.

"Princes prosper by iniquity, as the lion by the slaughter of the elephant."

In the same book, among the rules of the art of war, much is said of the use of the elephant. I extract only the following saying:

"The elephant, in the front of the army, serves the king, as no one else can do;

"The proverb calls him eight-weaponed with his own limbs."

These eight natural weapons are the trunk, the brow, the two tusks, and the four feet.

I am not able to say if any mention is made of the elephant in the oldest of the Indian books, the Vedas. In the laws of Manus (Menu) there is frequent mention of him, and one may perceive that he belongs to the objects which habitual observation has familiarized to the imagination. The worthy lawgiver advises that the maiden to be selected for a spouse, should have the graceful gait of a flamingo, or a young elephant. The figure of the elephant was used as a plaything for children. "As an elephant cut out of wood," so the saying goes, "as an antelope made of leather, even so is an unlearned bramin: these three things have nothing but the name." The tame elephant appears to have been a common article of private property, and there is a fixed penalty for killing it. Frequent mention is made of the use of the animal in war, and a passage in the Hitopadesa on this subject is borrowed from the laws of Manus. —Many religious usages are relaxed to the war class, that they may not be interrupted in their military exercises.—If a warrior has been present at funeral obsequies, he is purified by touching his arms, his charger, or his elephant. There are his nearest holy reliques.

In the introduction to the Ramagana, the capital city, Ayodhya, is delineated, and the elephants of the King Dasarathas circumstantially panegyrized. Their dwelling is in the mountains of Vindhya and Himavet. As with us the horse is celebrated for its pedigree, so are they sprung from the noblest race of their species, and distinguished by the luckiest marks. —These statements require a commentary, which is not found to be found in the English edition. The general meaning of the epithets bhadra, malla, mriga, two of which are sometimes joined together, perhaps to express two distinguishing marks united in the same animal, are well known; but in the application to the elephant, I only find the last explained. Mriga is generally the timid wild beast, particularly the antelope; then elephants with a white star so named. For this reason the elephant is called in the Hitopadesa, Karparatilaka. Tilaka is the figure which the Indians paint upon their brow, generally with reference to the worship of some deity; such elephants appear to be preferred for pomp. I have before my eyes an original picture representing the traveling equipage of a great princess: the two elephants upon which the standard bearers sit, have large white stars, which go down in a long stripe from the forehead to the trunk.

The expressions denoting the state of wild unruliness into which the tame elephant, chiefly in the season of the rut, again returns, are generally used in a good sense; not only matta, mad, wild with joy; but also prabhinna, raging—properly, one broken loose. —This periodical fury, during which the animal again feels its gigantic strength, has lately in Europe thrown terror into populous cities, and they have been obliged to have recourse to cannon as the only means of safety. In India, they know and possess the most efficacious remedy; the obedient elephants are employed to tame the outrageous ones, which are then bound and chained fast till the paroxysm is over; and it is well known the elephant, at the time of this periodical discharge, easily falls into this state, and must be carefully watched. As the principal object is always the use in war, the animal was prized for his courageous vigor. Accustomed in populous cities to see him wander about, only led by the hook of his driver, or quite at liberty, the Indians do not so easily take the alarm. It is a part of the pomp of a royal train, to have the elephants to prance behind the chariot of the monarch, in playful military movement, as with us noble horses are taught to curvet and stamp the ground with their hoofs.

And here the observation forces itself upon us, that in India, where for thousands of years there has been opportunity of making innumerable experiments, and the probability of propagating the elephant as a family heirloom could not have been overlooked, there was probably no inclination to continue the breed by these means for fear of degeneracy in point of strength and courage. If the elephant had been educated as a domestic animal, how would it have been possible to unfold his instinct for fighting, as in the great forests, when pressed by the necessities of nature? In these wilds, the elephants must live in herds, not only from social instinct, but for mutual defence; the male, when arrived at his full strength, may defy every danger, but the young brood would hardly grow up to maturity in any other manner.

Buffon's description of the peaceableness of the elephant in the wild state is somewhat exaggerated. We find in an old Indian poem, a representation of a nightly attack of a herd of elephants, which is certainly sketched after nature. A caravan, with all sorts of beasts of burden, horses, camels, elephants, is marching over the Vindhya mountains, and rests for the night on the banks of a clear, cool lake, covered with the blossoms of the lotus. Wearied with the journey, all are wrapped in deep sleep, when in the middle of the night there comes a herd of wild elephants to drink. As soon as they perceive the tame elephants, they rush upon them like an avalanche from the mountain, and slaughter them; they kill with their tusks, and trample underfoot the camels, the men, and make a terrible devastation. The whole description is of the sublime cast, and can only proceed from nature itself, seized upon with the true spirit of poetry.

The war elephants are certainly the allies of men against their free brethren. In the great driving hunts they surround the palisades, and drive back the wild ones that wish to break out. On these occasions we may perceive that the wild elephant has a hostile instinct against the tame one, for he attacks him even without provocation. —Perhaps he discovers by the smell his intercourse with man; and when the single male elephant is decoyed into the snare by the tame female, his instinct may perhaps be overpoised by the impulse of sexual desire.

The poets praise in various similes the social qualities of the animal. —The large male elephant compassionately caresses the female, which has been wounded by the poisoned arrow of the hunter, and falls down in pain; the female elephants, on the contrary, roar piteously when they see their tusked leader bound.[1]

We have the testimony of the ancients that this sympathy may be extended in a wonderful manner to the human species, and amongst others, the moving story of the Indian woman who had accompanied an elephant driver in the army of Antigonus, and dying in childbed, bequeathed her child to the care of the faithful elephant. —The elephant would always have the cradle to stand near him, and refused all sustenance when they took it away; he rocked it gently backward and forward, and drove off the flies with a tuft of straw when it slept.

The elephant is sensible of the approach of storm, and roars when the thunder comes rolling in the distance. The author of the Nalus has made a fine use of this circumstance. As the hero, with lightning's speed, enters the court of the palace where his beloved dwells, Damayana knows him by the thunder of his chariot; the beasts are deceived, the peacocks in the court scream, and the elephants in the stalls roar out with delight.

Another poet gives the following description: "The elephants of the forest, seized with desire, roar incessantly, in unison with the noise of the coming thunderclouds, their temples glisten like the pure lotus flower when the bees swarm round it, and sip its dew."

The raging elephant is often compared to a thundercloud; very naturally, on account of its gigantic bigness, its dark color, its powerful quick motion, and its threatening roar.

I have stated everything most worthy of remark of the extracts which I had made from the poets; in the sequel there will no doubt be opportunity of making additions. I will now subjoin some observations upon the productions of the mimic art.

Representations of the elephant are found upon the oldest Indian monuments that we are acquainted with. —Sometimes his colossal figure stands before the temples, hewn in separate stone; for instance, in the famous rocky cavern, upon an island near Bombay, to which the Portuguese gave, in consequence, the name of Elephanta. More frequently, however, it belongs to the buildings, as an inseparable part, and forms an architectural ornament. Here, upon the raised basis of a temple grotto, adorned in the manner of a frieze, lie rough draughts of elephants, one before the foot of each pillar, while above, upon the capital, a tiger is darting forward; there, upon frieze divided into compartments, heads of elephants are interchanged with leaping lions. Some quadrangular masses of temples, not underground, but hewn out of the natural rock upon the place itself, are entirely upborne by elephants, which, being turned outwards, three or four on each side, are arranged together, so that their bodies lose themselves behind in the bases. This idea seems to be taken from the elephants which support the world, and reminds us of a work of Phoenician art—the colossal brazen basin in Solomon's temple, which rested in the same manner upon twelve calves turned outwards.

The skill and boldness of conception with which the figure is exhibited will be evident from this rapid statement. With regard to the style of the execution, many of these ancient monuments are too much injured by the weather to permit a judgment to be passed upon it. From the delineations we possess, we could not with any certainty form an opinion: in the large English copperplates everything is sacrificed to the picturesque effect of the ruins, and much still remains to be wished for with respect to the architecture, and everything with regard to the figures with which the rocky walls of the temple are filled. Unless a person could transplant himself into a foreign mode of thinking, he would hardly at first feel inclined to do justice to the imitative art of the Indians, or of the Egyptians, in the execution of their animal figures. I have seen some of these in bronze, in which the true characteristic imitation of nature is not to be surpassed. I am even in possession of an elephant cast in bronze, about four inches high, of genuine Indian workmanship, in which the propor-tions of the general shape are quite exact; in some particular parts there is a failure, probably because it was necessary that the cast metal should be touched over again from a blunted form. We may also distinguish the manner of harnessing; the sumpter saddle above, with a round surface, is fastened upon a housing to the belly-girth, the breast-band, and crupper: on the shoulder-band is suspended a row of ball-shaped bells: a cap ornamented with tassels and strings of pearls covers the forehead: rings are stuck upon the tusks.

But we have much more minute information as to the sumptuous harness, which it was the custom in India to lay upon the elephants in solemn processions, in ancient times as well as now, from paintings in which the materials can be exhibited to the eye and the ornaments more finely executed. —There now lies before me an original picture, representing a prince seated upon an elephant. The aged, hoary-bearded monarch, his head surrounded with a glory; the driver riding upon the neck; the marching animal itself, are evidently portraits, and done with such an unassuming appearance of truth, that a Benozzo Gozzoli, or John of Fiesole, could not have made them better. The prince sits after the eastern fashion, in a sort of gilded box; the housing is of gold stuff, embroidered with flowers. Golden ornaments are attached to the girths, in the form of garlands: below the belly-girth hangs a bell, a pair of others upon the neck: a string with little golden balls or bells, a feminine ornamented, is bound round the heel of each foot: before the aperture of the ears hangs a chamaram, or white fly-lash, from the silk-haired tail of the grunting ox: a spot upon the temples is rubbed in with the dust of the red sandalwood: the cap on the forehead is bound with a double string, one of pearls the other of precious stones: on each of the tusks are stuck three golden rings. Their tips are made blunt from prudential motives, which I observe also on other similar figures: it would not do for a war elephant. All this is arranged in a very tasteful manner; but what is most worthy of remark, is the consideration that we see before us not only the custom of modern times, but also that of the ancient and most remote of all; for the heroic poems speak in the same manner of the splendid harness and ornaments of the elephant. It is a very appropriate trait in the history of Indian civilization, that a refined luxury of every kind carries us back into a remote antiquity, and that this luxury, which generally brings in its train a change of ideas, remains here in unison with the patriarchal and heroic manners: a phenomenon which only can be satisfactorily explained from the sacred character of the Indian legislation.

In animal figures, though everything in them cannot be of equal consequence, it is an important problem for the artist, especially for the sculptor, to borrow from nature those positions and motions, which, being in unison with the character, best unfold the shape of the limbs. The lion, all muscle, all activity and strength at the same time, may be represented lying, stooping, standing, striding, leaping; all these are favorable for sculpture. —A horse, on the contrary, in bronze or marble, standing still, would be always a stiff figure. The trot also is unfavorable, on account of the sharp angle which the stiff foremost legs makes with the other, as we may see in some works of the more ancient Grecian art. In times of a more refined taste, the Grecians have therefore always represented the horse either striding or leaping in the gallop. The elephant also would be most advantageously represented striding. In Indian bas reliefs and statues (for the large stony mass requires all the four supports) this is generally the case, and, indeed, in a peculiar manner; the resting foreleg is placed somewhat obliquely forward, the one raised to move is thrown backwards, just as in the fiery bulls of ancient art. I would always recommend to an artist, who had undertaken, as once Bernini did, to execute an elephant in brass or marble for a monument on a large scale, not to despise the study of the Indian originals, there being so few in Europe done from nature, in order to learn from them one or other modes of motion.

I might here speak of the fantastic figures of elephants, which are composed of all sorts of beasts or human forms. They are sufficiently worthy of observation, but do not strictly belong to our subject. Besides, it is time to close this dissertation, which has unexpectedly grown on my hands, that it may not swell to such a bulk as the laborious but not critical Elephantographia of the Graf of Hartenfels. —I only wish that my attempt to illustrate some points of the political and natural history of the animal by the collection of evidence may not be thought as fruitless as is, according to the Indian proverb, the growth of an elephant.

---

1. Barbarians only could make use of poisoned arrows in hunting; lawless mountaineers, such as have been in India from remote times, and still exist, and who are either the remains of the Aborigines or descendants of those who have been thrust out from society, or a mixture of both.

www.ingramcontent.com/pod-product-compliance
Lightning Source LLC
Chambersburg PA
CBHW070303290526
45791CB00003B/1060